W9-BVD-602

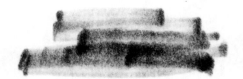

THE WAY PEOPLE LIVE

Life of a Roman Slave

Titles in The Way People Live series include:

THE WAY
PEOPLE
LIVE

Life of a Roman Slave

by Don Nardo

Lucent Books, P.O. Box 289011, San Diego, CA 92198-9011

Library of Congress Cataloging-in-Publication Data

Nardo, Don, 1947–
    Life of a Roman slave / by Don Nardo
        p.   cm. — (The way people live)
    Includes bibliographical references and index.
    Summary: Discusses aspects of slavery in ancient Rome, including
    becoming a slave, its privileges and perils, the use of slaves in farming,
    business, and public service, and the dark side of the institution.
    ISBN 1-56006-388-2 (lib. bdg.: alk. paper)
    1. Slavery—Rome—History—Juvenile literature. 2. Slaves—Rome—
    Social conditions—Juvenile literature. [1. Slavery—Rome.]
    I. Title.   II. Series.
    HT863.N37 1998
    306.3'62'0937—dc21   97-46715
                                                                       CIP
                                                                        AC

Contents

Discovering the Humanity in Us All

The Way People Live series focuses on pockets of human culture. Some of these are current cultures, like the Eskimos of the Arctic; others no longer exist, such as the Jewish ghetto in Warsaw during World War II. What many of these cultural pockets share, however, is the fact that they have been viewed before, but not completely understood.

To really understand any culture, it is necessary to strip the mind of the common notions we hold about groups of people. These stereotypes are the archenemies of learning. It does not even matter whether the stereotypes are positive or negative; they are confining and tight. Removing them is a challenge that's not easily met, as anyone who has ever tried it will admit. Ideas that do not fit into the templates we create are unwelcome visitors—ones we would prefer remain quietly in a corner or forgotten room.

The cowboy of the Old West is a good example of such confining roles. The cowboy was courageous, yet soft-spoken. His time (it is always a he, in our template) was spent alternatively saving a rancher's daughter from certain death on a runaway stagecoach, or shooting it out with rustlers. At times, of course, he was likely to get a little crazy in town after a trail drive, but for the most part, he was the epitome of inner strength. It is disconcerting to find out that the cowboy is human, even a bit childish. Can it really be true that cowboys would line up to help the cook on the trail drive grind coffee, just hoping he would give them a little stick of peppermint candy that came with the coffee shipment? The idea of tough cowboys vying with one another to help "Coosie" (as they called their cooks) for a bit of candy seems silly and out of place.

So is the vision of Eskimos playing video games and watching MTV, living in prefab housing in the Arctic. It just does not fit with what "Eskimo" means. We are far more comfortable with snow igloos and whale blubber, harpoons and kayaks.

Although the cultures dealt with in Lucent's The Way People Live series are often historically and socially well known, the emphasis is on the personal aspects of life. Groups of people, while unquestionably affected by their politics and their governmental structures, are more than those institutions. How do people in a particular time and place educate their children? What do they eat? And how do they build their houses? What kinds of work do they do? What kinds of games do they enjoy? The answers to these questions bring these cultures to life. People's lives are revealed in the particulars and only by knowing the particulars can we understand these cultures' will to survive and their moments of weakness and greatness.

This is not to say that understanding politics does not help to understand a culture. There is no question that the Warsaw ghetto, for example, was a culture that was brought about by the politics and social ideas of Adolf Hitler and the Third Reich. But the Jews who were crowded together in the ghetto cannot be understood by the Reich's politics. Their life was a day-to-day battle for existence, and the creativity and methods they used to prolong their lives is a vital story of human perseverance that would be denied by focusing only on the institutions of Hitler's Germany. Knowing that children as young as five or six outwitted Nazi guards on a daily basis, that Jewish policemen helped the Germans control the ghetto, that children attended secret schools in the ghetto and even earned diplomas—these are the things that reveal the fabric of life, that can inspire, intrigue, and amaze.

Books in The Way People Live series allow both the casual reader and the student to see humans as victims, heroes, and onlookers. And although humans act in ways that can fill us with feelings of sorrow and revulsion, it is important to remember that "hero," "predator," and "victim" are dangerous terms. Heaping undue pity or praise on people reduces them to objects, and strips them of their humanity.

Seeing the Jews of Warsaw only as victims is to deny their humanity. Seeing them only as they appear in surviving photos, staring at the camera with infinite sadness, is limiting, both to them and to those who want to understand them. To an object of pity, the only appropriate response becomes "Those poor creatures!" and that reduces both the quality of their struggle and the depth of their despair. No one is served by such two-dimensional views of people and their cultures.

With this in mind, The Way People Live series strives to flesh out the traditional, two-dimensional views of people in various cultures and historical circumstances. Using a wide variety of primary quotations—the words not only of the politicians and government leaders, but of the real people whose lives are being examined—each book in the series attempts to show an honest and complete picture of a culture removed from our own by time or space.

By examining cultures in this way, the reader will notice not only the glaring differences from his or her own culture, but also will be struck by the similarities. For indeed, people share common needs—warmth, good company, stability, and affirmation from others. Ultimately, seeing how people really live, or have lived can only enrich our understanding of ourselves.

The Nature of the Evidence

Slavery was an institution common to all ancient societies. Yet in no other single society in human history was that institution of such central importance than in ancient Rome. Indeed, slavery pervaded and helped to shape all areas of Roman life, including the home, agriculture, trade and industry, the arts, the law courts, and the government. The presence and productive output of a large population of freed slaves, or freedmen, also profoundly affected most aspects of Roman life. Many slaves achieved their freedom. However, while free in the strict legal sense, they did not enjoy the same social status as Romans who had been *born* free; rather, as a rule, freedmen were unable to rid themselves of the stigma of being servile and inferior, and they were rarely accepted as equals by free Romans. Because freedmen began as slaves and remained in many ways connected to the institution of slavery, the experiences of freedmen are integral to any examination of Roman slave life.

Reconstructing the everyday lives of Roman slaves and freedmen is not an easy task. This is because the evidence available to historians is often patchy, unclear, unreliable, biased, or just plain missing. More than fifteen centuries have passed since Rome ruled the Mediterranean world, and many of the written sources relating to slavery have disappeared. Of those sources that have survived, some are in the form of slave laws listed in the two major collections of Roman laws—the Theodosian and Justinian Codes, compiled in

the fifth and sixth centuries, respectively. These statutes provide a certain amount of useful information. One such law, for example, states that "whosoever harbors a fugitive slave in his house or on his land without the knowledge of his owner must return the slave and one like him or twenty gold pieces."[1] This law reveals that slaves sometimes ran away, that other slave owners sometimes took them in, and that slaves were valuable commodities. Yet it tells us nothing about how many, how often, or why slaves ran away, why people harbored them, how many harborers returned the slaves to their masters, or how commonly such harborers defied the law and faced prosecution.

Historians also learn about ancient slaves and freedmen from the surviving works of Greek and Roman writers. Some of these documents impart valuable information about slavery in passing, that is, while discussing another subject. In his discussion of noted Olympic wrestlers, for instance, the second-century A.D. Greek traveler Pausanias mentions that the athlete Nikostratos "came from a distinguished family and was stolen by Phrygian pirates . . . as a little baby."[2] This and similar accounts by other writers reveal that people were sometimes kidnapped and sold into slavery by pirates. Other documents refer more directly to slavery. The first-century A.D. encyclopedist Pliny the Elder discusses wealthy freedmen, one of whom owned 4,116 slaves.[3] And the *Satyricon*, a work by Pliny's contemporary Petronius, is filled with references to the lives and customs of slaves and freedmen.

But as valuable as they can be in some ways, the descriptions of slaves and freedmen in such writings also present historians with certain serious limitations and problems. First, most ancient writers dealt primarily with the lives of the rich, famous, and powerful; their references to members of the lower classes tended to be few, superficial, and concerned mainly with unusual or noteworthy examples and situations. As classical scholar Thomas Wiedemann puts it, "One of the problems about the literary evidence is that what was thought worth noting down was almost always what was exceptional."[4] Pliny's mention of the notorious slave owner is a perfect example. It would have been far more helpful to later ages if Pliny had investigated and recorded both the number of slaves in society as a whole and the average number of slaves owned by the members of various social classes; because he and other Roman writers failed to do so, modern historians are forced to make educated guesses about such numbers.

The example of Petronius's *Satyricon* illustrates other common problems with ancient writings about slavery. First, it is a work of fiction, a novel about the colorful, often comic adventures of three young men. Although most of the customs, situations, and character types described are likely based in reality, many are exaggerated and some perhaps fabricated for the sake of comic effect; and separating fact from fiction is sometimes difficult. This problem also affects modern readings of the plays of Plautus (third century B.C.); *The Golden Ass*, a novel by Apuleius (second century A.D.); and the satires of Juvenal (first century A.D.), all of which frequently refer to slaves and freedmen. These works were intended as entertainment, not as precise historical records; therefore their references to slavery must be interpreted carefully.

Another reason for exercising caution in interpreting Petronius's work is that, like most other noteworthy Greek and Roman writers,

A well-to-do Roman woman is attended to by her slaves. Most ancient writers concentrated on the lives of the upper class and said little about the experiences and problems of ordinary people, especially slaves.

The Nature of the Evidence

he was free and a member of the upper classes, and therefore had an automatic bias against slaves and freedmen. All highborn and most freeborn Romans readily accepted the idea that slaves were inferiors. They also agreed with the principle of the maxim stated by the second-century A.D. jurist Gaius, that "slaves are in the power of their masters; in all the nations the masters have the power of life and death over the slaves."[5] Even the most humane masters accepted that the use of force to control slaves was both necessary and correct. The great first-century B.C. orator Cicero, known for his fair and kind treatment of slaves and freedmen, wrote: "Severity must be employed by those who keep subjects under control by force, by masters, for example, towards their slaves, if no other way is possible."[6]

Thus, upper-class Roman writers recorded a reasonable amount of objective evidence—facts about the occupations, duties, conditions, rebellions, and punishments of slaves; but they did not understand and therefore failed to convey the *sub*jective evidence—what it felt like to *be* a slave. These privileged men could barely conceive of, let alone answer, such agonizing questions as those recently posed by University of Victoria scholar Keith Bradley:

> What, for instance was it like to be a captive of the Roman army and to know . . . that the only future you faced was to be butchered or sold off into servitude? . . . What did you feel when your wife and children were torn away and handed over to slave-dealers . . . to be sold on the block and never seen again? . . . Or what did it feel like to grow up as a slave . . . [and] gradually to come to realize that you were the symbol of everything that the powerful in society thought despicable, rotten and corrupt? . . . And what was it like to anticipate the lick of the lash, the clasp of the slave collar, the touch of the branding iron? To feel so desperate that you would run away and abandon all family ties and all the security of the household in an attempt to create a better life somewhere else, knowing all the time that you would be hounded, perhaps recaptured and returned to a life more miserable than the one you had left?[7]

A later European engraving depicts the great Roman orator Marcus Tullius Cicero, whose surviving letters contain comments about his relationshps with and feelings for his slaves.

Unfortunately, these and other similar essential questions about Roman slavery remain unanswered, for no accounts written by slaves about slavery, if any such documents ever existed, have survived. We do have a few scattered writings by freedmen, most notably the second-century B.C. playwright Terence and the first-century A.D. philosopher Epictetus.[8] But these works tend mainly to accept the institution of slavery as inevitable and offer few insights strictly from a slave's point of view.[9]

In the absence of subjective evidence, therefore, it becomes necessary for the reader to fill in the blanks when examining the lives of Roman slaves and freedmen. He or she must, at times, place him- or herself in the situation described and try to imagine how it would feel. Traditionalists object to this approach, arguing that it is unwarranted and potentially mislead-ing to try to reconstruct the psychology and emotions of one age using evidence from other times and places. Yet while the nature of slavery as an institution has unquestionably varied from one society to another, the human reaction—a slave's feelings of fear and indignity and desire for freedom—are apparently common to all. Bradley phrases it this way: "Modern historians and sociologists, knowing full well the need to make every allowance for particular variations in one society after another, have disclosed nonetheless the universalist features of slavery across time and space: to pretend otherwise is futile."[10]

The Brutal Reality of Supply and Demand: Becoming a Roman Slave

The Romans practiced slavery throughout their long history. What is more, members of all classes, even including slaves and freedmen, accepted the institution as an inevitable fact of life. Rome formally recognized and thereby helped to perpetuate this inevitability by carefully defining slavery, slaves, freedmen, and free persons in its laws:

> Slavery is an institution of the common law of peoples by which a person is put into the ownership of somebody else, contrary to the natural order.[11]

> The principal distinction made by the law of persons is this, that human beings are either free men or slaves. Next, some free men are free-born, others freedmen. The free-born are those who were free when they were born; freedmen are those who have been released from a state of slavery.[12]

Yet while slavery was a legal as well as physical reality throughout the Roman world, the numbers and nationalities of slaves varied widely in different eras and regions. The degree of Rome's dependence on slavery also varied, depending on the time period and region. The Romans had the most slaves and were most dependent on them between about 200 B.C. and A.D. 200. This period roughly encompassed the last two centuries of the Roman Republic, which lasted from

about 509 to 27 B.C., and the first two centuries of the Roman Empire, which supplanted the Republic and lasted until A.D. 476. Also, throughout Roman history, the largest concentration of slaves could always be found in Italy, the Roman heartland. Far fewer slaves were used in Britain, Gaul (what is now France and Belgium), Egypt, and other parts of Rome's empire. The story of how Rome acquired its slaves and how people found their way into servitude reveals some of the reasons for these variations.

Debtors and War Captives

In the first few centuries of the Republic, Roman territory was still confined to the Italian peninsula, so almost all Roman slaves were of Italian birth. A few of these early slaves were Romans who had fallen into debt; at the time, a creditor had the right to enslave someone who was unable to pay back a loan. The second-century A.D. Roman lawyer Aulus Gellius recorded the essence of the ancient law: "For a confessed debt . . . let thirty days be the legitimate time. Then let [the creditor] bring him [the debtor] to court. If he does not satisfy the judgment . . . let the creditor take him home and fasten him in stocks or in fetters [shackles]."[13] Apparently, in extreme cases the creditor could sell the debtor "across the Tiber," meaning to one of the many foreign

Newly acquired slaves await sale in a Roman slave market. In the early centuries of the Republic, most slaves were captives taken during Rome's many foreign wars.

peoples living beyond the Tiber River, originally one of the borders of Roman territory.

Another important early Roman slave source consisted of the captives taken in skirmishes with these neighboring Italian peoples. For example, the Romans fought the Etruscans, who lived north of Rome, with increasing frequency. And some early writings claim that the capture of the Etruscan stronghold of Veii in the early fourth century B.C. netted Rome some ten thousand captives. Not surprisingly then, war became the main slave source, especially after the Romans abolished debt-bondage in the late fourth century B.C.[14] At this point Roman society still had relatively few slaves, who were used mainly to supplement the free workforce; a typical slave-owning household probably owned only one or two slaves, and many families had none at all.

This situation steadily changed, however, as Rome's conquests and its acquisition of new territories accelerated. In the third century B.C.,

having conquered all of Italy, the Romans initiated the first of three devastating wars with Carthage, a powerful maritime empire centered in Tunisia in northern Africa. Rome took huge numbers of captives in these so-called Punic Wars—perhaps seventy-five thousand in the first conflict alone. From this time on, nearly all Roman slaves acquired as war captives were non-Italians. More importantly, by the end of the Second Punic War (218–201 B.C.), Roman society had become thoroughly dependent on slaves, in large part to fill a growing labor vacuum created by its military policies. Noted historian Michael Grant explains:

With so many free men away in the army, the role of slaves on the home front became more and more significant: they were employed in agricultural and industrial production on an unprecedented scale, without which the free recruits for the army could never have been raised and taken away."[15]

Generous Incentives for New Slaves

Sometimes, when it suited their purposes, the Romans did not enslave all of the war captives they took and offered generous incentives to those they did enslave. Here, from his Histories, *the second-century B.C. Greek historian Polybius tells how, after capturing the Carthaginian town of New Carthage during the Second Punic War, the Roman commander first allowed the citizens to return, free, to their homes; then he addressed the town's craftsmen, who were of more use to Rome.*

"He told the craftsmen that, for the moment, they were public slaves of Rome; but he proclaimed that if they cooperated and worked hard at their particular crafts . . . they would be given their freedom. He or-dered them to register their names . . . and appointed a Roman overseer for each group of thirty; there were about two thousand of them altogether. . . . From those who were left, he selected those whose strength, appearance and age made them most suitable and mixed them in with his ship's crews, so that he increased the total number of sailors by half. . . . He promised these men too that they would get their freedom if they cooperated and worked hard, once the war with Carthage had been won. By adopting this approach towards the captives, he made the citizens well disposed and loyal both towards himself and towards Rome generally, and he gave the craftsmen a great incentive to work because they hoped for their freedom."

In fact, the relationship between war and the institution of slavery became so important to the Romans that they defined it in legal

Wealthy Romans barter for a slave with Carthaginian merchants in the years between the Second and Third Punic Wars.

terms. "By the common law of peoples," stated one jurist, "those who have been captured in war and those who are the children of our slave women are our slaves." Another jurist further defined the connection between war and servitude: "The word for property in slaves (*mancipia*) is derived from the fact that they are captured from the enemy by force of arms (*manu capiantur*)." [16]

In the second and third centuries B.C., war continued to swell Rome's slave ranks as Roman armies ran roughshod over the Greek kingdoms of the eastern Mediterranean. Hundreds of thousands of captives from Greece, Asia Minor, Palestine, and other parts of the Near East flowed back toward Italy, most passing through Rome's chief marketplace for eastern slaves, the tiny Greek island of Delos. The situation was similar near the northern and western Roman borders; as many as 150,000 Germanic tribesmen were captured in 101 B.C. and perhaps half a million more when Julius Caesar conquered Gaul a few decades later. As with the Carthaginian and eastern prisoners, most of these German-born slaves ended up in Italy, where the majority of Roman aristocrats, each of whom could afford to buy many of them, resided. By the end of republican times, an estimated one-third of Italy's total population of 6 to 7 million consisted of slaves.[17]

Other Sources of Slaves

During these same centuries, piracy created a lucrative black market for slaves, supplementing the supply of war captives. Pausanias described a large-scale raid by pirate slave traders on the coast of Epirus (in northwestern Greece) in the late third century B.C. The pirates first pretended to befriend but then turned on the unsuspecting residents of the town of Methone: "Men and women went on to the ships to give them wine and to get things in exchange. And now the [pirates] had the effrontery to carry away many men and even more women; they stored them into the ships and sailed [away], leaving the city of Methone depopulated."[18] And the Roman historian Suetonius recorded that in the first century B.C., "bandit parties infested the roads," even in parts of Italy, kidnapping travelers, "whether free-born or not," and forcing them into "slave-barracks built by the [wealthy] landowners."[19] As a rule, the only

A Roman magistrate and a slave dealer oversee the sale of local natives captured during Rome's subjugation of Iberia (Spain).

In the climax of the Third Punic War, the Romans besiege Carthage, the prosperous and powerful city-state that had once controlled the western Mediterranean. At the conclusion of the conflict, the Romans killed most of the inhabitants and mercilessly enslaved the rest.

kidnap victims who escaped slavery were the wealthy and powerful, on whom the pirates made a larger profit by ransoming them off. This is what happened when a band of pirates captured Julius Caesar, then a brash young aristocrat, in 75 B.C.[20]

Other slave sources grew in importance as the Republic gave way to the Empire. The first two centuries of the Empire constituted a largely peaceful era (the *Pax Romana*, or "Great Roman Peace"), in which both war and piracy were less common and therefore no longer supplied Rome with the majority of its slaves.[21] Ordinary commerce and domestic slave-breeding now largely filled the gap. About the benefits to owners of *vernae*, or slaves bred in the household, scholar Harold Johnston comments:

> Such slaves would be more valuable at maturity, for they would be acclimated [accustomed to the master's house] and less liable to disease, and, besides, would be trained from childhood in the performance of the very tasks for which they were destined. They would also have more love for their home and for their master's family, since his children were often their playmates.[22]

During the early Empire, it was still a bit cheaper to buy than to breed slaves, so commerce probably supplied more slaves than breeding in this period. The city of Rome now became one of the great slave markets of the world, as slaves were imported from many of the imperial provinces and also from foreign lands such as Ethiopia, Arabia, and even faraway India. Many of those brought into Italy had already been slaves in their native regions and now merely exchanged masters; while others were captured by professional slave catchers not unlike those who plundered black Africans in the sixteenth through nineteenth centuries. Although these ancient slave catchers were seen as disreputable characters, the authorities usually turned a blind eye and tolerated them, since the products of their raids were an important supplement to other slave sources. Professor Bradley points out the brutal reality of supply and demand:

Evidence shows that slaveowners . . . were able to draw on several sources of supply that complemented one another and kept pace with demand, fluctuating from time to time in their relative standing one to another, but with no single source ever dominating the rest. The Roman slave supply was met from a combination of sources that commonly reinforced one another.[23]

The Number of Slaves in a Household

Because of the continued demand for slaves and the variety of sources meeting that demand, for a long time the ratio of slaves to free persons in the Empire remained high (perhaps one slave for every two or three free persons in Italy and one for every four or five in most other areas). Only in the last two centuries of

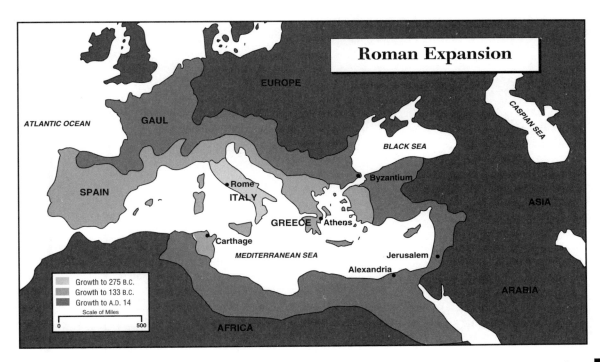

Duped by a Clever Slave Dealer

This excerpt from Pliny the Elder's Natural History *shows how some slave dealers managed to cheat customers, even powerful ones. In this case, Mark Antony—who briefly ruled Rome as part of the three-way coalition known as the Second Triumvirate in the late first century B.C.—was duped twice.*

"When Mark Antony was already a triumvir, the dealer Toranius managed to sell him as twins two particularly attractive slaves, one born in Asia and the other north of the Alps—they were that similar. But the fraud was brought to light because of the slaves' accents, and Antony angrily complained about the high price he had paid (50,000 *denarii*), amongst other things. But the clever trader replied that that was actually why he had asked for such a high price—there was nothing wonderful about twin brothers looking alike, but to find such a similar appearance in two persons who belonged to quite different races was really something that was beyond price; and he managed to make Antony think this [to be] so surprising . . . that although he . . . had just been in a terrifying rage, this man [Antony] ended up thinking that no other items that belonged to him were better symbols of his high status."

The Roman leader Marcus Antonius, more familiarly known by the modern version of his name—Mark Antony—was supposedly cheated twice by a crafty slave dealer.

the Empire did the demand for and numbers of slaves decrease somewhat, although by how much is uncertain. This was apparently due to a significant rise in the number of agricultural serfs, free tenant farmers who worked small plots of land owned by wealthy aristocrats; because the serfs did much of the work formerly done by slaves, fewer slaves were needed.

But the total number of slaves in society mattered little to individual slaves and their masters. Far more important to the everyday lives of both was the number of slaves in the household. For the master, the more slaves he had, the more leisurely his lifestyle and the higher his status; for the slave, having more slaves in the house might increase the chances for companionship and starting a family of his or her own; and, conversely, in a house with few slaves, each might be expected to carry more responsibilities and a heavier workload.

It is difficult to ascertain the number of slaves per household, partly because precise evidence is lacking and also because such numbers varied widely from one age and household to another. It appears that before the second century B.C., the average was one slave per household, except in the case of the wealthy, who could, of course, afford to keep more. This contention is supported by the indirect evidence of slave names. For a long time it was customary when naming a slave to take the Latin genitive of the master's name and to add to it the suffix *-por*, a slang version of *puer*, or "boy." Thus, a slave belonging to Marcus was called Marcipor, or "Marcus's boy," and Lucius's slave was Lucipor, a naming scheme possibly implying one slave per master.

With the large influx of slaves in the last centuries of the Republic, the average number per household sharply increased and slaves' names duly reflected the change. A master now gave each of his slaves an individual personal name. Often it denoted the

Wealthy Romans enjoy a banquet where they are waited on by slave servers and entertained by slave gladiators.

The Selling of Apalaustus

This is a translation of most of the text of a slave contract dating from A.D. 142, found in what was then the Roman province of Dacia (quoted in Lewis and Reinhold's Roman Civilization: Sourcebook II*).*

"Dasius, a Breucian, purchased and received by legal transfer for 600 *denarii* from Bellicus, son of Alexander . . . the boy Apalaustus, or whatever other name he may have, of Greek origin. . . . It is warranted [guaranteed] that this boy has been handed over in good health, that he is guiltless of theft or other delict [offenses], and that he is not a vagrant, a runaway, or an epileptic. And if anyone evicts from his possession the said boy in question or any part of him, thereby preventing the . . . purchaser or anyone to whom the said property may in the future belong from duly using, enjoying, having, and possessing it, Dasius the Breucian demanded the formal acknowledgment that in that case he would be duly paid in good coin double any amount thus evicted from his possession, and Bellicus, son of Alexander, formally promised that it would be paid. . . . Done [agreed to] in the camp town of Legion XIII Gemina on May 16 in the consulship of Rufinus and Quadratus. [Signatures of seller and witnesses are attached.]"

---

slave's original nationality or birthplace, so that a slave who hailed from Pharnaceia, a region bordering the southern shore of the Black Sea, might be called Pharnaces.[24] Also, the term *servus*, meaning slave, came to replace *puer;* and from the first century B.C. on, a slave's complete name consisted of his personal name, followed by the master's name, followed by the letter S, for *servus*.

Another piece of evidence supporting a larger number of slaves per household in the early Empire comes from the pen of the satirist Juvenal, who lived in the capital city in the first century A.D. Complaining about the difficulty of trying to make ends meet, he writes: "In Rome the problem's worse than anywhere else. Inflation hits the rental of your miserable apartment, inflation distends the ravenous bellies of your slaves."[25] This remark, along with other evidence, suggests that, at least in large cities, many middle- and lower-class people could afford to own more than one slave. Just how many more than one is unclear, but the case of

the well-known poet Horace offers a clue. Horace, a lower-middle-class gentleman, owned ten slaves, two of whom he kept in his city house, the other eight on the small country farm given to him by his wealthy patron, Maecenas. Perhaps a safe estimate for the number of slaves in a Roman household of average means is between two and ten.

Not surprisingly, members of the upper classes usually owned a great many more slaves. In one of his satires, Horace describes a spendthrift aristocrat known to waver between wealth and poverty: "Often he would keep two hundred slaves, often only ten."[26] This implies that ten slaves was considered a rather low number for a highborn person to own and that two hundred was a more respectable number. Several hundred slaves indeed appears to be the norm for an upper-class household: the first-century A.D. historian Tacitus tells of a public official named Secundus who owned four hundred slaves; and four hundred is also the number of slaves owned

In this drawing depicting a passage from one of Horace's odes, a master commands one of his slaves to pour him a cup of "ruby red wine."

by the wealthy freedman Trimalchio in Petronius's *Satyricon*. In such large households, it was customary for the sake of efficiency to divide the slave workforce into *decuriae*, divisions or groups of ten. The *Satyricon* alludes to this practice in a humorous incident involving Trimalchio, who has so many slaves he does not recognize them all:

Then he ordered a cook to be called in . . . and demanded in a loud voice, "What division do you belong to?" When the fellow made answer that he was from the fortieth, [Trimalchio asked,] "Were you bought, or born upon my estates?" "Neither," replied the cook, "I was left to you by Pansa's will."[27]

A few wealthy Romans had slaves numbering in the thousands. C. Caelius Isidorus, the rich freedman whom Pliny the Elder said owned 4,116 slaves, was a well-known example.

But when it came to slave owning, no private individual could compete with the emperors, each of whom, because of his extreme wealth and high position, typically owned up to twenty thousand slaves!

Public and Private Slave Sales

A great many of the slaves in these large households, at least in the early Empire, reached their masters via the auction block. Public slave auctions were supervised by officials called *aediles*, whose other duties included maintaining buildings and roads and organizing games and other public entertainment. The *aediles* imposed a sales tax on slaves imported into Italy, which meant that the government profited directly from the slave trade. As a rule, the *aediles'* assistants stripped the slaves naked, whitened their feet with chalk, and led them up onto the block, a raised platform on which they were plainly visible to all of the potential buyers. These buyers carefully examined the *titulus*, or placard, that hung from each slave's neck. The *titulus* served as both a list of the slave's qualifications and a warranty for the purchaser. Professor Johnston explains:

> If the slave had defects not made known in this warrant, the vendor was bound [by law] to take him back within six months or make good the loss to the buyer. The chief items in the *titulus* were the age and nationality of the slave, and his freedom from such common defects as chronic ill-health, especially epilepsy, and tendencies to thievery, running away, and suicide. In spite of the guarantee, the purchaser took care to examine the slaves as closely as possible. For this reason they were . . . made to move around, handled freely by the purchaser, and even ex-

amined by physicians. If no warrant was given by the dealer, a cap (*pilleus*) was put on the slave's head at the time of the sale, and the purchaser took all risks.[28]

In certain special cases, slaves were sold privately rather than on the open block. These slaves most often included those who were unusually handsome, beautiful, strong, highly skilled at some craft, and/or who could read and write. In such sales the buyer sometimes negotiated with a dealer, either reputable or disreputable, while other times he might transact the sale directly with a fellow citizen.

As might be expected, these more desirable slaves were the most costly. In general, the prices of slaves varied considerably from

Buyer Beware

An important Roman law protecting buyers in slave sales, listed in the Justinian Digest *(quoted in Lewis and Reinhold's* Roman Civilization: Sourcebook II), *reads as follows:*

"Any persons who sell slaves shall inform the purchasers of what disease or fault each has, who is a runaway or a vagrant, or is under indictment for a delict [offense]; and all this they shall openly and duly declare when they sell such slaves. . . . Likewise, if any slave has committed a capital offense, or has made any attempt to commit suicide, or has been sent into the arena to fight with wild animals, they shall openly declare all this at the sale; for we will grant a trial for such causes. Furthermore, if anyone is said to have sold contrary to these provisions knowingly and with malice of forethought, we will grant a trial."

*A group of slaves stands on display on a public auction block. Each slave wears
a placard (*titulus*) listing his or her qualifications.*

one time period to another and also according
to their type and perceived quality. For example, in the late third century B.C., the period
of the Second Punic War, an ordinary unskilled slave probably cost from 50 to 150 dinars (slang for *denarii*, common units of
Roman money).[29] Skilled workers seem to
have gone for 500 to 1,500 d. each; two children and a nursemaid sold together for 1,800
d.; and highly desirable slaves, such as strik-
ingly beautiful young girls and boys, cost from
2,000 to 6,000 d. These prices do not have
precise modern equivalents; but to help put
them in some perspective, in the period in
question, a Roman legionary soldier probably

earned about 100 d. per year, which was at
least two or three times what an average
lower-class worker made.

The prices of slaves were a good deal
higher in the early Empire. (For purposes of
comparison, soldiers now made 225 d. per year
and a moderately priced apartment in a tenement block in Rome went for about 500 d. per
year.) Horace mentions paying 500 d. for a
slave and implies that this was at the low end of
the price scale. Indeed, other evidence suggests that unskilled workers cost about 500 to
600 d. at the time, although a slave seen as having defects could be had for less. For instance,
one of the guests at Trimalchio's feast tells how

he snagged such a bargain: "He [the slave] has two faults, and if he didn't have them, he'd be beyond all price: He snores and he's been circumcised. And that's the reason he can never keep his mouth shut and always has an eye open. I paid three hundred dinars for him."[30]

Skilled slaves, on the other hand, cost at least 2,000 d. in the early Empire; and the bidding for educated slaves began at about 8,000 d. and could go well over 200,000 d. Suetonius tells of a wealthy aristocrat paying 175,000 d. for a highly educated teacher (and soon afterward setting the man free). The fact is that there was no limit to the cost if the buyer, for his own reasons, wanted the slave badly enough. As noted scholar F. R. Cowell remarks, "A slave, like a picture, a marble statue, or a rare book, was worth what any rich person was prepared to pay."[31]

Most senators and other members of the Roman aristocracy could well afford to spend such fantastic sums on slaves. The will of the first-century A.D. senator and lawyer Pliny the Younger, who owned at least five hundred slaves, disclosed his net worth at just under 5 million d.; by Roman aristocratic standards, that made him well-to-do but not rich. Fortunes of 25 million d. or more were not uncommon, which explains how such owners could buy and maintain hundreds or thousands of slaves.

Having invested a lot of money purchasing a slave (or raising the slave from infancy in the case of a *verna* born into the household), the master expected to receive a return on that investment. If the slave did not already possess a ready skill, he or she had to be trained for some useful task. As will be seen, there was never a shortage of such tasks. In a society that had become dependent on slave labor, there was literally a job for every slave and a slave for every job.

"Sir, I Do My Best": The Privileges and Perils of Household Slaves

By late republican times, slaves inhabited, worked in, and in large degree supported nearly every area and facet of Roman life. Yet slavery had originally developed within the framework of the family, or *familia*, the basic unit of Roman society. In the early Republic, before Rome became dependent on slave labor, most slave owners had only one or two slaves, who helped the household function more smoothly and often became loyal and trusted members of the family. Later, slavery spread to other social institutions, including many public ones, and slaves became differentiated into *servi publici*, public slaves, and *servi privati*, private slaves. Of a master's *servi privati*, his household slaves, known as *familia urbana*—especially the *vernae*, who had been born in the home— remained an integral part of family life.

From a slave's point of view, living and working in a private household had certain drawbacks, but also certain benefits. On the one hand, like all Roman slaves, the household slave had little or no control over his or her own life and fate. A slave was expected first and foremost to obey the master, to do whatever work he assigned without complaint, to go and come only as he allowed, and to satisfy his every whim, no matter how odd or degrading. This absolute power of a master over a slave was actually an extension of the authority held by a Roman family head, the *paterfamilias*, over the free members of his family. Noted scholar M. I. Finley explains:

The Latin *familia* had a wide spectrum of meanings: all the persons, free or unfree, under the authority of the *paterfamilias* . . . or all one's property [including slaves]; or simply all one's servants. . . . The *paterfamilias* was not the biological father but the authority over the household, an authority that the Roman law divided into three elements . . . *potestas*, or power over his children, his children's children and his slaves, *manus*, or power over his wife and his sons' wives, and *dominium*, or power over his possessions.[32]

Since a slave was seen both as the master's "child" and as his possession, his power over the slave was termed *dominica potestas*. This power gave the master the right to control a slave's entire life and to punish the slave at his own will and discretion. Thus, in the eyes of the law, a slave was no different than a sheep, a horse, or any other animal exploited by an owner.

On the other hand, in a society in which all slaves were exploited in this manner, household slaves were usually better treated and enjoyed more privileges and comforts than most other kinds of slaves. In particular, *vernae*, having grown up in the house, were often treated with nearly as much care and affection as the master's own children. As historian L. P. Wilkinson says, "Normal masters could hardly fail, even if half-ashamedly, to have a soft spot for characters they had seen toddling and growing up about the place."[33] Also, in the elegant surroundings of more well-to-do households, especially those of kind masters, slaves often ate and dressed better and were safer and more secure than most poor free Romans.

Household Slave Jobs

It is these larger, more comfortable households that historians know the most about, thanks in part to the surviving writings of well-to-do masters like Cicero and Pliny the Younger, who sometimes described their slaves in general or specific terms. These and other sources reveal that the *familia urbana* lived and worked in the master's town or city house, the *domus*, and that some of them accompanied him when he visited his country house, or villa (wealthier Romans often had two or more villas). Evidence also shows that the slaves in a large Roman household performed an extremely wide variety of tasks.

Such jobs ranged from the most unskilled and menial ones, like chambermaid and food server, to highly skilled and responsible ones, like accountant and financial manager. In smaller, simpler households there were naturally fewer tasks to perform, and the slaves were correspondingly fewer in number and less specialized.

One of the most common slave workers in larger households was the *atriensis*. In early Roman times, when most homes had few slaves, he was the head household slave, a sort of all-purpose butler who kept the master's accounts, did the buying, and supervised the work of other household slaves. Later, when large households with many slaves became common, their owners assigned duties such as accounting and buying to more specialized workers; this left the *atriensis*, himself now more specialized, with only certain supervisory duties.

Depending on the size of the house and staff, other slaves who commonly worked under the *atriensis* included the doorkeeper, or

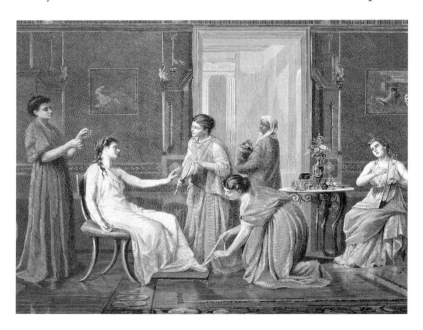

Dressers prepare an upper-class Roman lady for an outing. The richest homes, such as those of senators and other notables, were staffed by hundreds of such specialized slaves.

ostiarius; a dresser for the master, called an *ornator*, and a female dresser, or *ornatrix*, for the mistress; and a *paedagogus*, a slave who accompanied the master's son to school and supervised his behavior there. British scholar Kenneth Hughes lists these other essential slaves in a large home:

> Cooks, and other kitchen staff, under the control of a head cook; waiters to serve at table, attendants to assist the master and his wife to wash . . . [and] to wash and iron clothes, to heat water and prepare the baths, to trim the lamps and light them, to clean the house and its furniture . . . and generally to act as labor-saving machines in a hundred and one different ways.[34]

In very elite Roman households, such as those of the emperors and richest senators and military generals, the number, variety, and specialized nature of the *familia urbana* could be truly staggering. Such workers often included an *argentarius*, or silversmith; an *aurifex*, or goldsmith; a *capsarius*, or clothes folder; a *lanipendus*, or wool weigher; an *obstetrix*, or midwife; an *a purpuris*, or servant in charge of purple garments; an *architectus*, or architect (with a complete staff); an *a cyatho*, or cupbearer; a *praegustator*, or food taster; along with bakers, barbers, weavers, messengers, gardeners, grooms, actors, musicians, and pearl-, perfume-, and chair-keepers, to name only a very few![35]

From Pompous Retinues to Financial Managers

Besides performing their many and varied duties in and around the master's abode, some of the household slaves accompanied the master (and/or mistress) whenever he left the house. Displaying such a retinue of attendants was deemed a sign of social status, the larger and showiest being the most prestigious. Several members of larger retinues had specialized jobs. For example, if the mistress was traveling in a litter, or *lectica*, a legless couch carried by four or more male slaves, she had a female attendant who put her sandals on for her and placed the footstool for her to step on when getting off. Harold Johnston provides these other examples:

> Slaves [known as] *anteambulones* went before [the master and/or mistress] to clear the way, and pages and lackeys followed, carrying wraps or the sunshade and fan of the mistress, and ready to perform any little service that might be necessary. The master was often accompanied out of the house by his *nomenclator*, who prompted him in case he had forgotten the name of anyone who greeted him.[36]

Some Roman writers of more average means poked fun at such displays, which they found pompous. Juvenal ridiculed "that show-off Tongilius, who's such a bore at the baths with his mob of muddy retainers [retinue of slaves] . . . who has eight stout Thracian slaves humping the poles of his litter through the Forum [main square], to go shopping";[37] and Horace joked about a rich man's *nomenclator*: "If pomp and popularity make the fortunate man, let us buy a slave to call off names, to nudge our left side, and make us stretch out the hand [to important people] across the streets."[38] Despite such contemptuous remarks, slave retinues were not all show. Because there were no streetlights and criminal types often lurked in the shadows, the avenues and alleyways of Rome and other cities could be quite dangerous at night; so usually only the well-to-do, with their retinues of

Male slaves carry their owner through a luxurious garden. To advertise their social status, most well-to-do Roman masters took a retinue of servants wherever they went.

slaves armed with torches and weapons, dared to venture out after dark. When Juvenal took a chance and braved it alone, he was promptly mugged and beaten.

By far the most important and useful of an upper-class master's household slaves were those that helped him with his money and personal and professional business (some masters apparently entrusted these jobs mainly or solely to freedmen). Accountants, called *ratiocinatores*, kept track of income, payments, and debts, an essential and difficult task for a man who owned several houses, es-

tates, and/or other business interests. A higher-ranking accountant, the *dispensator*, oversaw the other accountants and all of the household's financial business. From Cicero's letters, we learn that in the late 40s B.C. a *dispensator* named Philotimus was in charge of his accounting staff, and that by about 46, Eros, the slave of Cicero's friend and correspondent Atticus, had taken over the job, aided to some extent by Tiro, Cicero's most trusted freedman.[39] In the *Satyricon*, the millionaire freedman Trimalchio had been a *dispensator* for his own master and now has *dispensatores* of his own. Well-to-do masters also used *procuratores*, slaves or freedmen authorized to act as their personal agents in business deals concluded outside the house.

Bonds of Loyalty and Love

That many rich masters gave *dispensatores* and *procuratores* nearly complete charge of their money and business affairs shows that a high degree of trust and loyalty often developed between owners and their personal slaves. This was particularly true in the case of *vernae*. By the early Empire, the term *verna* had gone beyond its original definition—simply a slave born in the house—to take on the added meaning of a proud position of responsibility and tried-and-true service. Cicero's friend Atticus used only *vernae* and carefully trained every one of them to read and write. And Cicero himself saw to the education of Tiro, to whom he had early taken a liking. In time, the trust invested in Tiro was so great that he handled all of the house's financial matters, scolded those who owed Cicero money and made polite excuses to Cicero's creditors, and obtained credit for the master from bankers. Even after Cicero freed him in 53 B.C., Tiro continued faithfully to serve his ex-master. The genuine respect and affection they shared is evident in this excerpt from a letter Cicero penned on hearing Tiro was ill:

> Your services to me are past all reckoning—at home, in the Forum, in the city, in my province; in private as in public affairs, in my literary pursuits and performances. You will surpass them all, if only I see you, as I hope I do, in good health.[40]

The mutual bonds of loyalty and love between Cicero and Tiro and between Atticus and some of his own slaves were not isolated cases. In a surviving inscription, for instance, a Roman master says he regards his slave as his son; and in another, a sixteen-year-old slave boy describes himself as his own master's son. Writing of the sudden death of a young woman from a wealthy family, Pliny the Younger remarks how much "she loved her nurses, her attendants and her teachers, each one for the service given her."[41] In Apuleius's *The Golden Ass*, when a mistress's servants perceive that the story's hero has made an indirect threat to her household, they close ranks, violently pummel him, and throw him out.[42] And the first-century A.D. court poet Statius left behind this moving rendition of a master's grief over the death of a *verna* he had adopted as his son:

A bust of Cicero, whose letters reveal his strong feelings of devotion for his slave and later freedman Tiro.

Shall I not mourn for you, dear boy? While you were alive I yearned not for sons; from your earliest birth my heart wrapped you round and would not let you go. I taught you words and sounds; as you crept on the ground, I bent down and lifted you up with my own hands to be kissed; when your cheeks were wet with tears I made you hide them in my welcoming arms and court sweet sleep.[43]

Testimony just as striking comes from the stories of slaves showing extraordinary loyalty, and even voluntarily dying for their masters. The famous Greek biographer Plutarch tells how Philip, the former slave of the great Roman general Pompey, tenderly cared for his ex-master's remains after Pompey's treacherous murder by Egyptian officials.[44] A few years later, while Mark Antony and his fellow

An idealized portrait of the Roman general Gnaeus Pompey, who, after his murder in Egypt, was buried by his still-loyal former slave.

triumvirs were murdering hundreds of their political opponents, several slaves, of their own accord, impersonated their condemned masters and died in their places.

In another well-known incident, recounted by the Romanized Greek historian Appian, during the brutal civil wars of the late Republic, a man named Restio was being hunted by his enemies. Suddenly, to his surprise, he found that one of his *vernae* had followed him. The slave kept Restio safe and fed in a cave until one day some hostile soldiers approached. Thinking quickly, the slave killed an old man, cut off his head, and presented it to the soldiers, claiming that it belonged to Restio, his former master, whom he had killed for the many beatings he had given him. "The soldiers took the head from him for the sake of the reward, and hurried to the city, where they discovered their mistake. [In the meantime] the slave got his master away and took him by ship to Sicily."[45]

Holidays, Marriage, and Other Privileges

It may ring strange in modern ears that people could show such love and devotion to those who had enslaved them. This apparent paradox becomes more understandable when one considers the prevailing beliefs of Roman times. First, slavery was universally accepted as a normal part of life, as evidenced by former slaves regularly and eagerly acquiring slaves of their own. Another common belief was that fate or the gods had willed some people to be masters and others to be slaves; thus, slavery was seen as a misfortune, rather than an evil, and most slaves felt no resentment toward their masters unless they were mistreated. Enslavement of free persons during raids on farms and towns by pirates, slave catchers, or soldiers was probably an exception. But people born into slavery, including Roman *vernae*, often felt grateful to their masters for feeding, clothing, and protecting them.

Household slaves were also grateful for certain privileges granted by custom and upheld by all but the cruelest of masters. Slaves were allowed to worship as they wished, freely admitted to religious temples, and considered to be under the protection of their household's personal deities, such as the *lares*, thought to keep the home safe.[46] Moreover, law recognized a slave's burial to be as sacred as that of a free person's.[47] And, with the master's permission, a slave could, along with free persons, join one of the *collegia funeraticia*, burial clubs that paid the funeral expenses of their members.[48]

Many (if not most) masters and their household slaves also celebrated together the Saturnalia, the December festival dedicated to Saturn, a major agricultural god (from which many Christmas customs are derived). One of the most eagerly anticipated of the Saturnalia's traditions was the day when masters and slaves switched places, the master obeying, waiting on hand and foot, and even enduring the chiding of his slaves. Horace devoted an entire satire to a slave lecturing and berating his master (all in good fun, of course) according to the custom of the Saturnalia. "I am weak [and] lazy," says the slave, Davus. "But you, since you are just the same and maybe worse, would you presume to assail me? . . . What if you are found to be a greater fool than even I?"[49]

Members of a Roman household happily celebrate the annual feast of the Saturnalia, in which one popular custom was for masters and slaves to switch places for a day.

It is likely that one reason so many masters participated in this custom was because they realized it was in their best interests. It not only made the slaves thankful for a welcome break from their usual routines, but also showed that the master was grateful for their service and thereby helped to maintain their loyalty. The same can be said for the Matronalia, celebrated on March 1, in which the mistress of the house switched places with her personal slaves, and for a general slaves' holiday widely celebrated on August 13.

Another privilege accorded many household slaves by their masters was marriage. To be more exact, such a union was an informal marital arrangement known as *contubernium*, meaning "cohabitation," for Roman law did not recognize the legality of actual marriage among slaves. In addition to this drawback,

any children of the union were seen as illegitimate and the property of the master. Yet the slaves who joined in such unions thought of themselves as husband and wife, as shown by the regular use of these terms in numerous surviving tomb epitaphs. And many masters encouraged the use of these terms. Like celebrating holidays with his slaves, promoting family life among his slaves was in a master's best interests because, as noted classical scholar Sarah Pomeroy suggests, "it improved morale and produced slave children who were the master's to keep in his household or to dispose of as he wished." About certain norms and restrictions of *contubernia*, Pomeroy adds:

> Slaves tended to marry other slaves, and were likely to marry within their master's

A roundel shows a married couple framed by the inscription "May you grow old together." Though Roman slave couples could not legally marry, many expressed similar touching sentiments in their tomb epitaphs.

Slaves of the Imperial Household

Here, from his well-known book Daily Life in Ancient Rome, *distinguished scholar Jerome Carcopino mentions just a few of the thousands of highly specialized slaves in the household of a typical emperor.*

"The emperor had as many categories of slaves to arrange and tend his wardrobe as he had separate types of clothes: for his palace garments the slaves *a veste privata*, for his city clothes the *a veste forensi*, for his undress military uniforms the *a veste castrensi*, and for his full-dress parade uniforms the *a veste triumphali*, for the clothes he wore to the theater the *a veste gladiatoria*. His eating utensils were polished by as many teams of slaves as there were kinds: the eating vessels, the drinking vessels, the silver vessels, the golden vessels, the vessels of rock crystal, the vessels set with precious stones. . . . A heterogeneous troop were employed to cook his food, lay his table, and serve the dishes, ranging from the stokers of his furnaces (*fornacarii*) and the simple cooks (*coci*) to his bakers (*pistores*), his pastry-cooks (*libarii*) and his sweetmeat-makers (*dulciarii*), and, including, apart from the majordomos [butlers] responsible for ordering his meals (*structores*), the dining-room attendants (*triclinarii*), the waiters (*ministratores*) who carried in the dishes, the servants charged with removing them again (*analectae*), the cupbearers who offered him drink and who differed in importance according to whether they held the flagon (the *a lagona*) or presented the cup (the *a cyatho*)."

familia. With permission, a slave might marry a slave from another *familia* or a free person. However, if a male slave married a female outside his master's *familia*, the master lost the profit that might be gained from the offspring, since the children belonged to the mother if she were free, or to her master if she were a slave.[50]

That such marriages between male slaves and free women became increasingly common and that many slave owners were disturbed by the trend is implied by the enactment of a law in A.D. 52, under the emperor Claudius, discouraging these unions. According to Tacitus, "Claudius proposed to the Senate that women marrying slaves should be penalized. It was decided that the penalty for such a lapse [in her honor] should be enslavement if the man's master did not know, and the status of a freedman if he did."[51] Thereafter in such cases, the woman and any children produced by the union became the slaves of her lover's master.[52]

Spending, Saving, and Investing

A great many Roman masters also granted their slaves the privilege of owning property, generally part of the *peculium* arrangement. Legally speaking, the *peculium*, consisting of money or property given to a slave by his or her owner, still belonged to that owner; in general practice, however, the slave had complete use of and control over it. There were many ways a slave might acquire a *peculium*. Some masters gave their slaves regular allowances, while others awarded them periodic tips and gifts for doing exceptional work or favors. It was also common practice for a master to allow his slaves to sell the remains of his feasts for their own profit and for a slave to hire himself out to other masters, paying his own master part of the earnings and pocketing the surplus. Some of the shrewder and more skilled slaves earned their *peculia* through business ventures. The esteemed scholar R. H. Barrow explains:

> The slave who made his master's business yield profits, to his own profit too, very often, had a keen sense of the best use to make of his own money. Often he reinvested it in his master's business or in enterprises entirely unrelated to it. He could enter into business relations with his master . . . or he could make contracts with a third person. He could even have [financial assistants] to manage his own property and interests.[53]

Slaves spent their money in many of the same ways that free people did. Buying gifts for relatives and friends was common; and custom dictated providing gifts for the master and members of his family on various special occasions. In the opening scene of Terence's play *Phormio*, a slave complains that such obligations are unreasonable:

> My great friend . . . Geta [another slave] came to [visit] me yesterday. . . . I hear his master's son has got married, so I suppose he's scraping up something for a gift to the bride. Unfair I call it, the have-nots always obliged to give to the rich. Poor old Geta struggled to save this little by little from his rations [*peculium*], denying himself his pleasures, and now she'll make off with the lot, never stopping to think of the labor it

cost him. Then he'll be stung for another present when she has a child, and after that there'll be birthdays and an initiation ceremony, all needing presents, and the mother takes all—the child is only the excuse for the present.[54]

Some slaves undoubtedly used up part or all of their savings on little comforts and luxuries, ranging from extra food and clothes, to burial club fees and tomb inscriptions, to prostitutes.[55] In the *Satyricon*, Trimalchio tells of one of his slaves buying a suit of armor and a comfortable chair "with his own money."[56] Evidence shows that more frugal slaves invested part of their *peculia* in valuable assets such as land, houses, livestock (often along with grazing rights), and shops. Such property became part of a slave's accumulated *peculium*, to be added to or invested as he or she wished. However, because the *peculium* legally belonged to the master, a slave could not sell it or give it away without the master's permission.

Another asset commonly acquired by slaves as part of their *peculia* took the form of slaves of their own. The slave of a slave was known as a *vicarius* (*vicaria* if female), who generally addressed his owner in the same way his owner addressed his own—as *dominus* (lord) or *magister* (master). The numbers of *vicarii* owned by slaves is unclear; but it appears that most household slaves who owned slaves had one, or perhaps two at most. As might be expected, slaves living in very wealthy households, especially that of the emperor, had more. Some slaves used their *vicarii* as helpers or attendants, while others hired them out as helpers to shopkeepers, millers, restaurant owners, and so on, which earned a profit and further increased the value of the *peculium*.

The size and value of the savings of household slaves must have varied greatly.

The majority, especially those of slaves in homes of average or less than average means, were probably meager; however, as will be seen later, some slaves saved enough to buy their freedom; and an exceptional few actually attained considerable wealth. When the emperor Julian visited Constantinople in A.D. 361, for example, he expressed amazement at meeting a slave barber from the imperial household who earned, in addition to an annual salary and bonuses, enough daily income to feed himself and his pack animals twenty times over.[57]

Exploitation of Slaves

In spite of the fact that many Roman household slaves had tolerable or even good relationships with their masters and enjoyed

According to the fourth-century A.D. historian Ammianus Marcellinus, Julian (pictured), the last pagan emperor of Rome, was amazed at the hefty earnings of an imperial slave.

certain privileges, such as marriage and spending money, it must be remembered that they still lacked their freedom. Law and custom recognized and supported the slave's status as inferior. And even the kindest, most generous masters routinely exploited and disciplined their slaves. This was a natural and expected part of the slave-owning institution; for while owners might admit that slaves were human beings, they saw them first and foremost as property, investments, and labor-saving devices. Also, because private slaves were part of the *familia* of the *paterfamilias*, an owner viewed them, even the adults, as children who required strict guidance and training. As he saw fit, therefore, he disciplined and punished them, often in the same ways he did his own children. Revoking privileges, boxing the ears, and flogging were among the most common forms of discipline for slaves, although some masters employed more brutal forms of punishment, such as chaining, branding, starving, breaking the ankles, or even castration.

Just as abusive as physical punishment was the calculated and often coldly casual exploitation of a slave's captive condition. Most slaves did not mind working normal jobs, even difficult ones. But just as they could not choose their master or residence, neither could they choose when, where, and at what job they worked. Moreover, Roman society regularly assigned them its most wretched and dangerous tasks; and for fear of punishment they had to obey.

Another way some masters took advantage of their household slaves' servile position was to exploit them sexually. Today, we see this as a serious form of abuse; but apparently throughout most of their history the Romans, both masters and slaves, accepted it as a natural occurrence, something expected of a slave. In the *Satyricon*, for example, Trimalchio asserts that "I was my master's 'mistress' for fourteen years, for there's nothing wrong in doing what your master orders; and I satisfied my mistress, too."[58] Though this is an example from fiction, it mirrors reality; for matter-of-fact references to sex between masters and slaves appear in the writings of many ancient writers.[59] Attitudes about such behavior began to change, however, in Rome's last century or so, when Christianity became the Empire's official religion. Christian leaders condemned it as immoral, along with all other sexual relations outside of marriage. The fifth-century Christian writer Salvian asks:

What will the morals of slaves have been like, when the morals of the head of the household had sunk as low as that? How corrupted will the slaves have been, when their masters were so utterly corrupt? . . . These masters didn't just provide a provocation to behave wickedly, but an unavoidable necessity, since slave women were forced to obey their immoral owners against their will; the lust of those in a position of authority left those subjected to them with no alternative.[60]

One of the cruelest ways masters exercised the power they held over their slaves was by "selling them away." A slave could be sold to another master at a moment's notice and with little or no warning, sometimes having to leave behind family and friends. In *The*

His House a Country for His Slaves

That a Roman master could feel genuine sympathy for and a shared humanity with his slaves is evidenced by this sensitive and moving excerpt from one of the surviving letters of Pliny the Younger (8.16, translated by Betty Radice). Keep in mind that Pliny was an extraordinary individual and, by his own admission, more compassionate than the average slave owner.

"I have been much distressed by illness amongst my servants, the deaths, too, of some of the younger men. Two facts console me somewhat, though inadequately in trouble like this: I am always ready to grant my slaves their freedom, so I don't feel their death is so untimely when they die free men, and I allow even those who remain slaves to make a sort of will which I treat as legally binding. They set out their instructions and requests as they think fit, and I carry them out as if acting under orders. They can distribute their posses-sions and make any gifts and bequests they like, within the limits of the household: for the house provides a slave with a country and a sort of citizenship. But though I can take comfort from these thoughts, I still find my powers of resistance weakened by the very feelings of humanity which led me to grant this privilege. Not that I would wish to be harder of heart; and I am well aware that some people look upon misfortunes of this kind as no more than a monetary loss, and think themselves fine men and philosophers for doing so. Whether they are in fact fine and philosophic I can't say, but they are certainly not men. A true man is affected by grief and has feelings, though he may fight them; he allows himself to be consoled, but is not above the need of consolation. . . . Even grief has its pleasure, especially if you can weep in the arms of a friend who is ready with approval or sympathy for your tears."

Golden Ass, Apuleius includes an incident in which some household slaves decide to run away rather than face the prospect of a new owner.[61] And in her informative book about Roman women, scholar Jane Gardner mentions several examples of Roman slave families breaking up due to sale or the bequest of their owner in his will; among them was a second-century A.D. slave woman separated from her ten-month-old twins, who ended up in the custody of the master's daughter.[62]

The Reality of Submission

Thus, the life of a slave in an average Roman household had both ups and downs. A slave could expect both privileges and perils—more of the former and fewer of the latter if he or she worked hard and behaved. Indeed, obedience was the only path to a reasonably happy life for a slave; for the ultimate reality of Roman slavery, no matter how just and kind the master, was the slave's submission, which the master exploited in numerous ways for his own gain. In Terence's play *The Girl from Andros*, a slave's speech to his owner perfectly summarizes the precarious and vulnerable position in which all slaves found themselves:

The ultimate reality for slaves was that, like the servers at this banquet, they had no choice but to submit to the will of their masters.

As your slave, sir, it's my duty to work hand and foot, night and day, and risk my life if only I can be of service to you. If things don't always go according to plan, you only have to forgive me. My efforts may not be successful, sir, but I do my best. Of course if you like, you can think up something better yourself and get rid of me.[63]

A Tool Endowed with Speech: Slavery on a Roman Farm

Rome began as a farming society, and agriculture remained the principal basis of its economy and the wealth of its aristocracy throughout its long history. Adding to these factors the picturesque beauty of the Italian countryside, it is not surprising that urban and rural Romans alike had a strong emotional attachment to the land and country life. As scholar Garry Wills phrases it, "Romans always had a sharp nostalgia for the fields. Even their worst poets surpass themselves when a landscape is to be described."[64] Yet such idyllic and idealized literary views of the fields were mainly those of the upper classes who did not have to work in them. Most of the laborers on large agricultural estates were slaves owned by absentee landlords who lived in the cities; and even some of the smaller farmers had a similar arrangement, as seen in the case of Horace and his eight country slaves.

In contrast to the slaves of their townhouses, the *familia urbana*, the country slaves belonging to Horace and other Roman landowners were termed *familia rustica*. These rural workers were of two types. Some were groundskeepers who maintained the extravagant gardens, parks, game preserves, and fishponds that surrounded their masters' country villas. Because these slaves were not used to turn a profit, and also because many of them were highly skilled (at landscaping, cultivating flowers, and breeding and keeping fish and birds), they often enjoyed a status

equal to that of trusted household servants. Of a lower status, less skilled, far more numerous, and more characteristic of the term *familia rustica* were the slaves who toiled on the farming estates. The major commodities they produced included wine, olive oil, cattle (mainly for use as draft animals and for dairy products), pigs (pork was the Romans' favorite meat dish), sheep, honey (the main food sweetener), and timber.[65]

A Bleak Existence

Much of what is known about these slave farmworkers comes from the writings of three Romans: Marcus Porcius Cato, a soldier-statesman of the late third and early second centuries B.C. who wrote a farmers' manual titled *On Agriculture*; Marcus Terentius Varro, a first-century B.C. scholar whose *On Landed Estates* describes the management of large farms; and Lucius Junius Columella, a first-century A.D. estate owner who penned a book on farm management. These writers paint a generally unflattering and bleak picture of farm slaves and their lives. The skill and intelligence of such workers were seen as secondary to their strength and endurance, the jobs they performed were usually menial and monotonous, and they appear to have led more difficult, grayer lives than their counterparts in the city. Considering these factors, it

This drawing depicts a Roman slave working in his master's fields. Such lower-class rural workers usually led difficult and monotonous lives.

is not surprising that disciplining slaves was a bigger problem on farms than in the city. In describing farm life, Cato, Varro, Columella, and other ancient sources frequently refer to "lazy" and "dishonest" slaves, the chaining of slaves, and slave dungeons.

In the late Republic and early Empire, some rural slaves worked on small plots owned and managed by free independent farmers, carrying on the tradition of early Roman times. However, the majority of *familia rustica* were attached to the large ranches and estates owned by wealthy aristocrats or the government. These estates, called *latifundia,* had grown up in the wake of Rome's wars with Carthage and the Greek kingdoms, driving many small farmers out of business and increasing the number of slaves on the land. The late, great modern scholar A. H. M. Jones provided this thumbnail sketch:

The Roman aristocrats . . . were acquiring vast money fortunes from the exploitation of the empire, and investing them in land. The peasant proprietors of Italy were hard hit by long-term military service, and were compelled to sell their plots. Great estates thus grew up at the expense of small holdings, and as slaves were very cheap, the owners used them in preference to free labor.[66]

Indeed, the profit motive made it a given that large farms would exploit such free labor; and owners automatically factored in the cost of slaves when purchasing new tracts of land, as illustrated in a letter of Pliny the Younger in which he discusses the possibility of buying an estate adjoining his own:

The chief point for consideration is this. The land is fertile, the soil rich and well watered, and the whole made up of fields, vineyards, and woods which produce enough to yield a steady income if not a very large one. . . . [The property] will have to be set up and given a good type of slave, which will increase the expense.[67]

Since the vast majority of landlords like Pliny were absentee, another automatic expense of a farm business was maintaining a reliable on-site manager, or *vilicus* (also translated as steward or bailiff). In fact, Cato, Varro, and Columella all agreed that the key to making a *latifundium*, or even a smaller farm, turn a profit was the selection of a competent, trustworthy manager. The *vilicus* could be either a free tenant farmer (a *colonus*) or a slave. Columella held that in most cases it was better to have one's own slave run the estate, probably because harder work and more loyalty could be expected from the slave, a member of the master's *familia*, than from an unrelated tenant:

You will always get a higher return from an estate you look after yourself than from tenants—and you will even get a higher return if it is looked after by [your own] manager, unless this slave is particularly incompetent or corrupt. And if he does suffer from either of these vices, there can be no doubt that he generally does so . . . as a result of a mistake on his master's part, since his master could have made sure that he was not put in charge in the first place and that he was removed if he had already been appointed.[68]

Only when an estate was located at a very great distance from the master's townhouse, said Columella, was employing a tenant *vilicus* better. Here, his reasoning reflected the common Roman belief that slaves, even slave managers, were likely to be inefficient and untrustworthy when not regularly and tightly supervised:

But when the farms are a long way away, so that the head of the household finds it difficult to visit them, then any kind of cultivation by free tenants is preferable to that of slave managers. . . . They [the slaves] may hire out oxen and not pasture other cattle properly and not plow properly and claim that they have sown far more seed than they in fact have and not look after what they have sown to make it grow properly, and lose a lot of the harvested grain during threshing as a result of theft or incompetence. . . . The result is that neither the manager nor the slaves do their work properly and the reputation of the estate declines.[69]

Qualifications of a Good Manager

Whether or not most landowners followed Columella's advice and visited their estates on a regular basis is unknown; in any case, the majority of their *vilici* were slaves.[70] Owners naturally selected such managers with great care and always kept an eye out for slaves who showed managerial potential. According to Cato, who was a strict and conservative owner, a good manager has to be able to maintain strict discipline among the workers. And he must be ready to punish a slave who has committed some infraction "in proportion to the damage he has caused." At the same time, the manager must not mistreat the workers and should reward their good work, "so that the others have an incentive to work well too." Also, Cato writes, an effective manager must remain sober at all times and, in order to

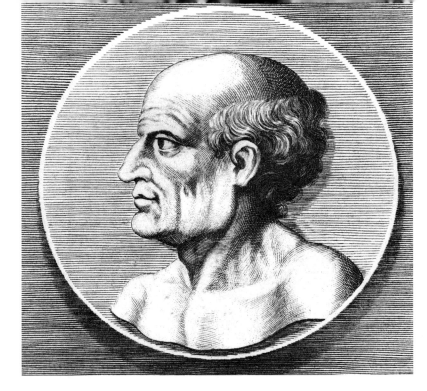

Marcus Porcius Cato, a conservative slave master, left behind a farmer's manual containing much detailed advice about how to maintain strict discipline among farm slaves and thereby run a prosperous and profitable estate.

keep a close eye on the farm, never go out to dinner or get involved in religious activities, "except those of the Compitalia [a January ceremony in which the staff set up an altar to purify the farm for the coming year], and those at the household hearth [such as the *lares*]." Cato maintains further that the *vilicus* must

> keep the slaves at their work and make sure that the master's orders are put into effect; he must not think that he is wiser than his master . . . he must lend no one money without his master's orders . . . he should frequently go through the accounts with his master . . . he should not want to buy anything [for the farm] without his master's knowledge, nor to keep anything secret from the master . . . he must take pains to know how to carry out every agricultural operation. . . . If he does these things, he will be less keen to

go out, his health will be better and he will sleep better. He must be the first to get out of bed, and the last to go to bed. Before that he must see that the farm is shut up, that everyone is asleep in their proper place, and that the animals are provided with fodder.[71]

Columella lists other qualities of a good slave *vilicus*, strongly emphasizing that it is best not to fill the position with one of the household slaves from the city. These servants, he says, are too used to sleeping a lot, attending the theater and chariot races, playing dice on the street corner, and frequenting bars and brothels, and they "dream of this nonsense all the time." Instead, Columella asserts, it is better to use someone who grew up on a farm and is therefore used to the long hours and hard work typical of farm life. Columella also underscores the importance of the manager's age:

He should no longer be a young man, since this will detract from his authority to command since old men don't like to obey some youngster; nor should he have reached old age yet, or he will not have the stamina for work of the most strenuous kind. He should be middle-aged and fit and know about agriculture, or at least be so dedicated that he will be able to learn quickly.[72]

Qualifications aside, as is true in all professions in all ages, some managers were highly effective and others only average or even inept. The best were those able to temper efficiency, organization, and strict enforcement of the master's rules with fairness and human decency. That a *vilicus* named Hippocrates, who managed a farm on Italy's eastern coast, was able to do so inspired his workers to honor him with this funerary inscription: "To Hippocrates, manager of Plautus; [from] the rural slaves over whom he exercised authority with moderation."[73] Another *vilicus* received a similar memorial from his owner, inscribed on a monument in Rome: "To the spirits of the Dead. To Sabinianus, a manager and a good and most faithful person. [From] his mistress Memmia Juliana."[74] By contrast, some managers must have been a good deal less faithful. Cicero describes a *vilicus* selling timber, equipment, and livestock behind the master's back, sending the master a small portion of the profits, and pocketing the rest.[75]

Farmworkers and Their Jobs

Of the slaves who worked under a slave *vilicus*, one of the most important, both to him and the estate, was his female companion, or *vilica*. Her function was apparently twofold—to keep the manager satisfied and happy, and therefore more apt to discharge his duties faithfully, and also to aid him in those duties. Columella describes her not only as a laborer, expected to do spinning, weaving, and other traditional women's work, but also as a nurse in charge of a small on-site hospital. "What she must continually be careful about," he states,

is to go round once the slaves have left the farmhouse and look for anyone who ought to be out working in the fields; and if she finds any malingerer inside, who has escaped the notice of her husband . . . she must ask why he is not at work and find out whether he has stayed behind because he feels ill or because he is lazy. If she finds that this is the case, she must immediately take him to the sickroom, even if he is only pretending to be ill; for it is worthwhile letting someone exhausted by his work take a day or two off and look after him, rather than force him to work excessively so that he really does become ill. . . . She should occasionally go and open up the sickroom even if there aren't any patients there, and clean it so that it is in an orderly and healthy state to receive anyone who may fall ill.[76]

The other slaves managed by the *vilicus* were numerous and their tasks highly varied. One of the most important jobs was driving the oxen that pulled the plow. According to Columella, a plowman, or *arator*, needs a muscular physique and a loud voice to "give him the necessary authority over his oxen." Yet he should also know when to go easy on the beasts, so that they last longer, another reminder of the importance of maintaining the master's profit margin. Also, "of all agricultural activities, plowing is least exhausting to a tall man, since he is able to stand up straight and rest his weight on the plow handle."[77]

In contrast, "vineyards do not need tall men," Columella says, "but rather broad and powerfully built ones." But more importantly, because dressing the vines takes more skill and judgment than the average farm job, vine dressers, or *vinitores*, have to be intelligent. Unfortunately, these quicker-witted slaves tend also to be *improbi*, "rascally fellows," who have a tendency to cause trouble; and "that is why vineyards are often worked by slaves in chains."[78]

Not necessarily less intelligent, but certainly of a lower status than plowmen and vineyard workers, were herdsmen and shepherds, whose occupation was seen as one of the most undesirable on an estate. *Opiliones*, sheepherders, and *pastores*, general herdsmen, usually led solitary lives in remote pasture lands, spending long hours and days away from family and friends; and they were regularly exposed to weather extremes and attacks by wild animals and bandits. Varro supplied the following qualifications for the job:

> For larger stock you need older men, for smaller stock even boys will do; but with regard to both groups, those who work along the cattle trails must be stronger than those who can go back to the farmbuildings on the estate every day. . . .

Roman cowhands were almost always slaves who led lonely lives in remote pastures, where they were also vulnerable to attacks by wild animals and outlaws.

Those who look after animals should be required to spend the whole day pasturing their flocks . . . [and] everyone is to spend the night with his own flock. They should all be under the charge of a Chief Herdsman; he should preferably be older and also more experienced than the others . . . but he must not be so much older as to be unable to put up with the hard work. . . . For neither old men nor boys easily put up with the hardships of the cattle trails along steep and rugged mountain sides.[79]

Some of the other farm jobs usually performed by slaves included those of *fosseres*, or diggers, who excavated furrows between vines and trees (which were too deep for the plow), as well as irrigation and drainage ditches; *putatores*, pruners and trimmers; *saltuarii*, boundary keepers, who patrolled, maintained, and guarded an estate's walls, fences, and natural borders; along with pig keepers, sheep shearers, stable boys, and so on. Columella stresses that each slave should specialize in a single job, "so that everyone doesn't do the same thing." Otherwise, "no one thinks that any particular job is his own responsibility," the slaves will become lazy, and "when work done by many has been done badly, it is impossible to identify who is re-

Like Puppies or Colts

This excerpt from Plutarch's Life of Cato (*in* Plutarch: Makers of Rome) *summarizes Cato's view, one probably shared, more or less, by most well-to-do estate owners of his era (early second century B.C.), that farm slaves were and should be treated basically as commodities with which to turn a profit.*

"Cato possessed a large number of slaves, whom he usually bought from among the prisoners captured in war, but it was his practice to choose those who, like puppies or colts, were young enough to be trained and taught their duties. None of them ever entered any house but his own, unless they were sent on an errand by Cato or his wife, and if they were asked [by a neighbor] what Cato was doing, the reply [per Cato's orders] was always that they did not know. It was a rule of his establishment that a slave must either be doing something about the house, or else be asleep. He much preferred the slaves who slept well, because he believed that they were more even-tempered than the wakeful ones, and that those who had had enough sleep produced better results at any task than those who were short of it. And as he was convinced that slaves were led into mischief more often on account of love affairs than for any other reason, he made it a rule that the [male slaves] could sleep with the women slaves of the establishment, for a fixed price, but must have nothing to do with any others. . . . [For his own gain] he would also lend money to any of his slaves who wished it. They used these sums to buy young slaves, and after training and teaching them a trade for a year at Cato's expense, they would sell them again. Often Cato would keep these boys for himself, and he would then credit to the slave the price offered by the highest bidder. He tried to encourage his son to imitate these methods, and told him that to diminish one's capital was something that might be expected of a widow, but not of a man."

sponsible." In addition, the various kinds of workers should be grouped into *decuriae*, since it is easier to keep watch over a group of ten workers, "while a larger crowd can escape the control of the overseer as he leads the way"; and also because "in groups of more than ten . . . individuals will not consider that the work has anything to do with them personally if they are part of a large crowd."[80]

Restraint, Regulation, and Discipline

Columella's references to workers attempting to avoid work, chained vineyard workers, and the importance of "the control of the overseer" underscore the often high degree of restraint, regulation, and strict discipline imposed on farm slaves. Along with Cato and Varro, he stressed that slaves should not be brutalized or mistreated. But this policy stemmed more from worries that mistreatment might harm morale, lessen productivity, and thereby reduce the owner's profits, than from concerns for the slaves as feeling human beings. The view that slaves were mere property, little different than other "things" found on an estate, is reflected in Varro's breakdown of farm tools into three categories. The first can speak, he says, another is inarticulate, and the third is speechless. "That [category] endowed with speech includes slaves, the inarticulate includes cattle, and the speechless wagons."[81]

Cato's famous statement about selling surplus or useless goods even more coldly emphasizes the common view of slaves as merchandise affecting a farm's bottom line—profitability. On inspecting the estate, he says:

> The head of the household should examine his herds and arrange a sale. He should sell . . . any wine and grain that is surplus to needs; he should sell any old oxen, cattle or sheep that are not up to standard, wool and hides, an old cart or old tools, an old slave, a sick slave—anything else that is surplus to requirements.[82]

In his *Life of Cato*, Plutarch provides further insights into Cato's treatment of farm slaves:

> It was a rule of his establishment that a slave must either be doing something about the house, or else be asleep. . . . He used to invite his friends and colleagues to dinner, and immediately after the meal he would beat with a leather thong any of the slaves who had been careless in preparing or serving it. . . . If ever any of his slaves were suspected of committing a capital offense, he gave the culprit a formal trial in the presence of the rest, and if he was found guilty he had him put to death.[83]

Not all Roman estate owners were as stern and pitiless as Cato, and many must have agreed with the harsh criticisms leveled by Plutarch:

> I regard his [Cato's] conduct towards his slaves in treating them like beasts of burden, exploiting them to the limits of their strength, and then, when they were old, driving them off and selling them, as the mark of a thoroughly ungenerous nature, which cannot recognize any bond between man and man but that of necessity. . . . Kindness and charity . . . may be extended even to dumb animals. . . . We ought never to treat living creatures like shoes or kitchen utensils to be thrown away when they are broken or worn out in our service, but rather cultivate the habit of behaving with tenderness and consideration towards animals, if only for the sake of gaining practice in humanity when we come to deal with our fellow-men.[84]

Cato Demands an Accounting

Here, from his famous treatise On Agriculture *(quoted in Lewis and Reinhold's* Roman Civilization: Sourcebook I), *Cato emphasizes both the wide range of menial tasks on a Roman farm and the expectation that the slaves should, like machines, keep busy at them through all their waking hours, rain or shine, even on holidays.*

"When the head of the household comes to the farmhouse . . . he should make the rounds of the farm. . . . When he has learned in what way the farm work has been done and what tasks are finished and what not finished, he should next day summon the foreman [*vilicus*] and inquire how much of the work is done, [and] how much remains. . . . After he has been informed on these points he should go into an accounting of the day's work and [what was done on which] days. If the work accomplished is not made clear to him, and the foreman says he has pushed the work hard, but the slaves have not been

well, the weather has been bad, [or] the slaves have run away . . . when he has given these and many other excuses, then bring the foreman back to an accounting of the farm tasks and of the day's work spent on them. When the weather was rainy, [tell him] what work could have been done in spite of the rain: the storage jars could have been washed and tarred, the farm buildings could have been cleaned out, the grain shifted, the manure carried out and a manure pile made, the seed cleaned, the ropes mended and new ones made; the slaves should have mended their patchwork cloaks and hoods. On festivals [holidays] they could have cleaned old ditches, repaired the public road, cut briars, dug the garden, weeded the meadow, made bundles of the small wood cut in pruning, dug out thorny hedges, broken up the spelt [grain] into grits, and made the place neat. When the slaves were sick they should not have been given as large an allowance of food."

"There Are Less Risks in Being Tame"

Yet even those owners who agreed with this sentiment and refrained from beating, killing, or callously discarding their slaves still expected those slaves to work diligently and help the farm turn a profit. Just as children and animals required a certain amount of discipline, went the conventional wisdom, so, too, did slaves. And even in the comparatively enlightened era in which Plutarch wrote (the late first and early second centuries A.D.), owners continued to work their farm slaves hard and to mete out appropriate discipline. Columella, who wrote his farm treatise when

Plutarch was a young man, advocated supplying farmhands with protective clothing so that they could continue to work outside even during storms and frosts. And it is Columella who suggested chaining vineyard workers, although this practice appears by his time to have been on the decline. Pliny the Younger, also a contemporary of Columella, commented that he never chained his estate slaves, nor did any of his neighbors.[85]

An exception was chaining slaves to punish them for breaking the rules. Evidently there had evolved by this time a thin but well-defined line between acceptable discipline or punishment and unacceptable abuse in the eyes of farm owners and society as a whole.

Thus, chaining a slave was seen as an acceptable form of discipline as long as the shackles did not damage the skin and the slave was well fed and clothed and had the right to complain about poor treatment. The same went for confining a rule breaker in the farm prison, or *ergastulum*.[86] According to Columella:

> There are some things that every careful man recognizes: that he must inspect the slaves in the farm prison to check that they're properly bound. . . . The head of the household should inspect this type of slave . . . carefully, and make sure that they are not being maltreated as regards clothing and other rations . . . and are more vulnerable to suffer injustice and also become more dangerous if they have been badly treated as the result of anyone's sadism or greed. That is why the master should ask both them and those who are not chained up . . . whether they are being treated in accordance with his instructions, and he must himself taste their food and drink to see that it is acceptable, and check their clothing, their fetters, and their footwear. He must frequently give them an opportunity to complain about anyone who makes them suffer as a result of cruelty or dishonesty. I personally will sometimes punish those

Aided by a horse, farm slaves work a primitive water pump. Such backbreaking work was the daily norm for slaves on Roman estates.

Friendly Manipulation

In this tract from his surviving agricultural treatise, On Agriculture, *Columella tells his readers that a master might find it useful at times to converse and even to joke with his farm slaves, mainly in an effort to manipulate them into working harder and more efficiently.*

"One should address those rural workers who have not behaved improperly in a friendly way more frequently than one would one's urban slaves. When I realized that such friendliness on the master's part relieved the burden of their continual labor, I often joked with them and allowed them to joke more freely. What I do quite often nowadays is discuss some new piece of work with them as though they were more knowledgeable than I am, and in this way I can find out what each one's attitude is and how intelligent he is. And I've noticed that they are much more willing to start a piece of work when they think that they've been consulted about it and that it was actually they who first suggested it."

responsible for justifiable complaints in the same way as I will severely punish those who incite the slaves to disobedience.[87]

Columella and other owners who followed these disciplinary policies undoubtedly saw themselves as fair and just masters. After describing these policies, Columella adds, "Conversely, I will reward those who work hard and diligently." He goes on to say that

if the head of the household behaves justly and carefully in this way, he will find that his patrimony [the worth of his estate] increases greatly . . . [and] that discipline [among his slaves] will remain good when he reaches an old age, and, however infirm he becomes with the years, he will never be scorned by his slaves.[88]

This, of course, is the one-sided opinion and wishful thinking of a free and privileged Roman. What his slaves whispered behind his back will never be known; but it is likely that they followed his rules less from gratitude for his "justice" and more from the practical realization that on a farm the most privileged and least punished slaves were those who did not make waves. According to the slave adage recorded in the first century B.C. by the ex-slave Publilius Syrus: "There are less risks in being tame."[89]

"Vulgar" but Indispensable: Slaves in Business and Public Service

Beyond the self-contained little worlds of Roman households and farms, slaves were involved in nearly all of society's workaday trades, industries, and business concerns. Some were *servi privati*, either serving as assistants, apprentices, or laborers for masters who owned or ran businesses, or assigned by absentee owners to run such businesses themselves. Others were *servi publici*, public slaves owned and exploited by the Roman state, individual towns, or the emperor.

Some free Romans worked alongside slaves in these capacities. But they were almost always freedmen or lower-class freeborn persons, for upper-class Romans viewed such work as disreputable and beneath their dignity. Cicero's statement of this attitude is the best known:

> Now in regard to trades and other means of livelihood, which ones are to be considered becoming for a gentleman and which ones are vulgar . . . [the vulgar ones include those] of all hired workmen whom we pay for mere manual labor . . . for in their case the very wage they receive is a pledge of their slavery. Vulgar we must consider those also who buy from wholesale merchants to retail directly. . . . And all mechanics [craftsmen] are engaged in vulgar trades.[90]

The reason for this condescending attitude toward the trades and menial work in general is not completely clear. Perhaps, as Michael Grant suggests, over time the high prominence of slaves in such fields "helped to degrade industry and trade in people's minds."[91] Also, most free Romans came to feel that taking orders from someone else was the act of a slave. "Free-born Roman citizens," states

A Roman potter plies his trade. Most upper-class Romans saw such menial labor as vulgar and beneath their dignity.

Vulgar and Acceptable Ways of Making Money

In this famous section of his treatise De Officiis, *or "On Duties," Cicero describes working in trades on a small scale as "unbecoming to a gentleman" and a form of slavery, even when performed by free persons; whereas buying and selling on a large scale is more socially acceptable, especially if the riches gained in this manner are invested in land, the basis of the nobility's wealth.*

"Now in regard to trades and other means of livelihood, which ones are to be considered becoming for a gentleman and which ones are vulgar, we have been taught, in general, as follows. First, those means of livelihood are rejected as undesirable which incur people's ill-will, as those of tax-gatherers and usurers. Unbecoming to a gentleman, too, and vulgar are the means of livelihood of all hired workmen whom we pay for mere manual labor, not for artistic skill; for in their case the very wage they receive is a pledge of their slavery. Vulgar we must consider those also who buy from wholesale merchants to retail directly; for they would get no profits without a great deal of downright lying; and . . . there is no action that is meaner than misrepresentation. And all mechanics [craftsmen] are engaged in vulgar trades; for no workshop can have anything liberal about it. . . . Trade, if it is on a small scale, is to be considered vulgar; but if wholesale and on a large scale, importing large quantities from all parts of the world and distributing to many without misrepresentation, it is not to be greatly disparaged. Nay, it seems to deserve the highest respect, if those who are engaged in it . . . make their way from the port to the country estate. . . . Of all the occupations by which gain is secured, none is better than agriculture, none more profitable, none more delightful, none more becoming to a free man."

scholar Keith Hopkins, "traditionally disliked the idea of working as long-term employees at the beck and call of other free men (except in the army). . . . [They] apparently felt that a permanent job restricted their freedom of choice, constrained them like slaves."[92]

Because of this prejudice toward work, most Roman tradesmen, craftsmen, industrial workers, and business functionaries were slaves or freedmen. And most free Romans also shunned "servile" positions in administration, including the staffs of the provincial governors and even the emperors. Ironically, because some of the positions on these staffs entailed considerable responsibility and authority, a number of the public slaves and freedmen who held them came to wield more influence than most of the freeborn Romans who saw them as social inferiors.

Slaves in Shops and Businesses

The most common arrangement in shops, factories, and other private businesses and institutions was that of a freedman (or sometimes a freeborn person) managing a staff composed primarily of slaves. The freedman might own the shop and the slaves; or he might manage them for an absentee owner, most likely his former master. In either case, the slaves filled most of the individual occupations, both general and specialized, and did most of the work.

Take the example of the barbershop, or *tonstrina*, a common fixture of Roman cities and towns, which was similar in many ways to a modern beauty shop, except that it catered to men.[93] Statements by ancient writers, as well as surviving examples of barbers' instruments (or drawings of them), indicate that the customers had their hair cut and/or curled, their faces and/or head and eyebrows shaved, and their nails manicured. In smaller shops, one or two slaves probably performed all of these services, or aided the manager in performing them. Larger shops likely displayed the same tendency toward specialization seen among household slaves, with some slaves specializing in shaves, others in manicures, and so forth.

The same situation prevailed in many other private establishments, including those of shoe- and bootmakers, fullers (who finished cloth and cleaned clothes), brick makers, tailors, jewelers, carpenters, cloth merchants, metalworkers, food vendors, and numerous others. Slaves who worked in bathhouses, as attendants (*balneatores*), furnace-operators (*fornacatores*), or in other capacities were especially common. Roman cities and towns also featured large numbers of *pistores*, who both milled and baked bread. Whether employed in actually making the bread, or in selling it at a shop called a *pistrinum*, apparently nearly all were slaves or ex-slaves; and it is therefore not surprising that Cicero expressly described their profession as vulgar.

The well-preserved remains of a Roman bakery, much like the reconstruction pictured here, were discovered in the ruins of the city of Pompeii, near modern Naples. A typical bakery employed several slaves.

Social status aside, such slaves were indispensable to shops and businesses, and by extension to the Roman economy in general. This was mainly because their labor was so cheap (not completely free, of course, because most received some form of *peculium*). This factor, combined with smart business practices and a quality product or service, made some shop owners very successful. A number of freedmen amassed small fortunes this way, as the literary sources attest. Juvenal, for example, puts these words in the mouth of a brash freedman who sees himself just as worthy as his supposed betters: "My five shops bring in four hundred thousand [*sestertii*], see? So I qualify for the gentry. . . . I have more stashed away in the bank than any Imperial favorite."[94]

The relationships between such owner-managers and their slaves, like those in the household and on the farm, likely varied from case to case. At least in situations in which the owner worked closely with and/or apprenticed a slave, bonds of friendship, and even love, must have developed often. A surviving tomb inscription records the grief of a jeweler over the death of his young assistant:

> Shed for this lad you passer-by, a tear. Twelve years of boyhood's springtime he had lived, his master's joy, his parents' fondest hope, whom cruel he has left to

A slave delivers foodstuffs and other supplies to one of the local snack bars (thermopolii) *that were common in Rome and other Italian cities.*

lasting pain. He knew to work with cunning craftsmanship at necklaces, and set in softened gold all kinds of jewels. Pagus was his name. But now, a bitter grief, within the grave as dust, a corpse without a name, he lies.[95]

Slave Managers

Had this young jeweler, Pagus, lived, his owner would probably eventually have entrusted him with running the shop when he himself was away, for giving slaves this degree of responsibility was a common practice. And some slaves actually managed shops and other businesses on a full-time basis for their absentee masters. Such a slave bore the title of *institor*, a term describing any person, free or not, appointed by a business owner to manage that business. Thus, a *vilicus* who managed a farm for its owner was a kind of *institor*.

In the commercial world, slave *institores* had charge of a wide range of enterprises, from shopkeeping and money lending, to buying and selling all manner of merchandise, including slaves. Inns were commonly run by slaves, for instance. In his agricultural treatise, Varro advises landowners to make extra money by building inns where their lands touch main roads and to appoint slaves to manage them. A Roman inscription found near Philippi, in northern Greece, bears the epitaph of such an innkeeper, one Vitalis, who had been adopted by his master: "I ask you travelers to forgive me if I have ever given you short measure. It was to help my father. I beg you, by the gods above and the gods below, to let me commend my father and mother to you."[96]

While some slave *institores*, like Vitalis, held permanent positions in inns, shops, and the like, others carried out short-term com-missions or contracts for their masters, including the transaction of business deals. Keith Bradley cites the case of a slave named Hesicus, who himself became financially involved in a deal transacted for his master, a freedman named Evenus:

In the summer of A.D. 37 Hesicus acted for his owner . . . when a certain C. Novius Eunus, a dealer in foodstuffs, borrowed 2,500 *denarii* from Evenus. . . . Beyond this, however, Hesicus also made a loan of 750 denarii to the food merchant in his own right, using assets . . . that were in effect his own [his *peculium*]. Thirteen months later the second loan had not been fully cleared and new terms were fixed for payment of the outstanding balance. Now, however, Hesicus was no longer the slave of . . . Evenus, but of the emperor. He had changed hands, but his capacity to act as an independent financial broker had clearly not been affected.[97]

A slave *institor* could also act as a real estate agent, as shown in an advertisement found at Pompeii (the Roman town buried and largely preserved by a volcanic eruption in A.D. 79):

To rent, from the first of next July, the Arriana Polliana block of buildings, the property of Gnaeus Alleius Nigidius Maius, containing shops with the rooms over them, splendid chambers, and a house. An interested tenant should apply to Maius's slave.[98]

The building trades constituted another common area in which owners contracted out their slaves for various specific short-term jobs. Information about one such contract comes from Justinian's *Digest*, which mentions

Public Slaves as Prison Guards

In A.D. 111, the emperor Trajan appointed Pliny the Younger as his special representative to investigate administrative corruption in the province of Bithynia, in Asia Minor. During his stay there, Pliny corresponded regularly with the emperor, among their letters this exchange concerning public slaves used as prison guards (from Betty Radice's translation).

"Pliny to Trajan:
I pray you, Sir, to advise me on the following point. I am doubtful whether I ought to continue using the public slaves in the various towns as prison warders, as in the past, or to put soldiers on guard-duty in the prisons. I am afraid that the public slaves are not sufficiently reliable, but on the other hand this would take up the time of quite a number of soldiers. For the moment I have put a few soldiers on guard alongside the slaves, but I can see that there is a danger of this leading to neglect of duty on both sides, when each can throw the blame on the other for a fault they may both have committed.

Trajan to Pliny:
There is no need, my dear Pliny, for more soldiers to be transferred to guard-duty in the prisons. We should continue the custom of the province and use public slaves as warders. Their reliability depends on your watchfulness and discipline. For, as you say in your letter, if we mix soldiers with public slaves the chief danger is that both sides will become careless by relying on each other. Let us also keep to the general rule that as few soldiers as possible should be called away from active service."

---

the legal case of a plasterer, or *tector*, who fell from a scaffold while on a job. The question raised was whether the slave's owner or the man for whom the slave was working was responsible for the damages; and the judgment was that if there was a prior understanding that the slave would be working on a scaffold, the owner assumed the risk and had to absorb the damages.[99]

"We Deserve What We Get"

Slaves worked in many other occupations, most of which freeborn Romans as a rule tried (but did not always manage) to avoid. Perhaps the lowliest, filthiest, and most dangerous of these jobs was mining. The ownership of mines varied—some belonged to the state, others were leased by the state to individuals, and still others were privately owned. Similarly, the miners were of various types, some of them free laborers hired by a contractor, some criminals condemned to spend a number of years or life in the mines, and others slaves assigned by the mine owners. Their tasks and the horrendous working conditions they faced were captured by the first-century B.C. Greek historian Diodorus Siculus:

They [the owners] purchase a multitude of slaves whom they turn over to the [mine] overseers . . . and these men [the miners], opening shafts in a number of places and digging deep into the ground, seek out the seams of earth which are rich in silver and gold; and not only do they go into the ground a great distance, but they also . . . run galleries [tunnels] off at every angle. . . . [They] produce for their masters revenues in sums defying belief, but they themselves wear out their bodies both by day and by night in the diggings under the earth, dying in large numbers because of the exceptional hardships they endure. For no respite or pause is granted them in their labors, but compelled beneath blows of the overseers to endure the severity of their plight, they throw away their lives in this wretched manner. . . . Indeed, death in their eyes is more to be desired than life, because of the magnitude of the hardships they must bear.[100]

Another unsavory and dangerous profession largely manned by slaves and criminals was that of gladiator, or arena fighter. Of the noncriminals who fought as gladiators, the vast majority were slaves (occasionally free men, usually freedmen, volunteered); and of these slaves, most were war captives or the victims of pirates and slave catchers. As Professor Grant explains, "In inscriptions recording lists of gladiators, the free are normally distinguishable from the slaves by the form of their names. Thus an inscription from the island of Thasos [in Greece] shows 2 free men to 10 slaves."[101] Most of these slaves probably died on the job; however, a combatant who won many victories might receive an honorable discharge (becoming a *rudiarius*, or retired gladiator) and with it his freedom.[102]

Certain occupations dominated by slaves carried significantly higher status and prestige, among them those of ship captain, doctor, teacher, and personal secretary. Because they were very educated and skilled, these kinds of slaves were very valuable and always in demand. Keith Hopkins tells how they filled a culture gap that existed between Rome and the lands it conquered and administered, especially Greek lands:

Gladiators battle to the death in a Roman arena. Most of these warriors were slaves who hoped to earn their freedom by winning many matches; however, most died on the job.

The Romans admired and wanted to imitate the culture of the conquered [eastern Mediterranean lands]. But imitation required refined education and the exercise of skills, in which Romans had no experience. To fill the gap, Greek-speaking philosophers, teachers, and doctors were brought to Rome. Slavery was one of the chief methods of recruiting the highly cultured to work in Roman Italy. The sophistication of Rome as the cultural capital of [its] empire, depended considerably on educated, foreign-born slaves.[103]

Some of these educated slaves worked in their masters' households; but a number of them engaged in commercial activities, fulfilling contracts outside the home for their masters. In the cases of ship captains and doctors performing such work, the health and very lives of many free Romans often rested in the hands of these slaves, a reality that disturbed at least some members of the upper classes. Commenting on the reluctance of free Romans to learn such jobs, Pliny the Elder admonished, "We deserve what we get [if a slave doctor kills us], since none of us wants to learn what he has to do for his health."[104]

Keeping Rome's Apparatus in Motion

While privately owned slave doctors, teachers, and ship captains served selected members of the public, *servi publici* served society as a whole and did so at the state's, municipality's, or emperor's expense. Public slaves, especially imperial ones (those owned by the emperor), enjoyed the highest social status and the most opportunities to make money and wield influence of any category of Roman slave. They also rated certain special privileges not accorded

other slaves. For instance, most public slaves were allowed to dispose of one-half of their property in their wills in any manner they wished (whereas all of the property of other slaves who died reverted to their masters); and male imperial slaves could marry free women and have legitimate children by them.

The status and privileges of public slaves derived in part from their connection to the government and the imperial throne, which were society's most prestigious institutions. Also, once Rome had allowed itself to become dependent on slave labor, the jobs these slaves performed were so essential that society could not have continued functioning without them. Public slaves were involved in every area of state and local administrative work; they comprised the backbones of the staffs of state priests, tax collectors, the consuls (chief administrator-generals during the Republic, who retained certain powers and prestige during the Empire), the *aediles*, and the town magistrates; they built and maintained roads, temples, amphitheaters, aqueducts, and other public structures; they oversaw the public markets, the corn supply, and the public dole (the government's free handouts of corn and other foodstuffs to the poor); and they carried the state's mail; maintained its libraries, mints, treasury, and financial accounts; and acted as foremen for its mines and quarries. In short, public slaves kept the vital apparatus of the Roman realm in motion.

Unfortunately, few documents have survived describing in any detail the duties, lives, and accomplishments of these public servants.[105] The major exception is *The Aqueducts of Rome*, a technical work on the complicated water system supplying the capital city, written by Sextus Julius Frontinus (A.D. 40–104). A distinguished administrator (formerly the governor of the province of Britain), Frontinus received the important job of water commis-

Slaves of the Water Commission

In his treatise The Aqueducts of Rome, *Frontinus gives the following information about the duties and wages of the two slave gangs under his authority.*

"Both gangs are divided into several classes of workmen: overseers, reservoir-keepers, inspectors, pavers, plasterers and other workmen; of these, some must be outside the city [Rome] for purposes which do not seem to require any great amount of work, but yet demand prompt attention; the men inside the city at their stations at the reservoirs and fountains will devote their energies to the several works, especially in cases of sudden emergencies, in order that a plentiful reserve supply of water may be turned from several wards of the city to the one afflicted by an emergency. . . . The wages of the state gang are paid from the state treasury, an expense which is lightened by the receipt of rentals from water-rights, which are received from places or buildings situated near the conduits, reservoirs, public fountains, or water-basins. This income of nearly 62,500 *denarii*, formerly lost through loose management, was turned in recent times into the coffers of [the emperor] Domitian; but . . . [the emperor] Nerva restored it to the people. . . . The gang of Caesar gets its wages from the emperor's privy purse [imperial finance office], from which are also drawn all expenses for lead [for pipes] and for conduits, reservoirs, and basins [that make up the system of aqueducts]."

sioner from the emperor Nerva. The water commission had been created a century before by the first emperor, Augustus, who had appointed his friend Marcus Agrippa to head it. According to Frontinus, Agrippa

> kept his own private gang of slaves for the maintenance of the aqueducts and reservoirs and basins. This gang was [later] given to the state as its property by Augustus, who had received it in inheritance from Agrippa. . . . There are [now] two of those gangs, one belonging to the state, the other to Caesar [the emperor]. The one belonging to the state is the older. . . . It numbers about 240 men. The number in Caesar's gang is 460.[106]

Frontinus goes on to explain that each slave gang is divided into specialized groups, including managers, inspectors, and various kinds of craftsmen to make any necessary repairs. During an emergency, he says, these extremely well-trained slaves rush into action, diverting water from various regions of the city to the region in need. He also mentions

Tombs like these, lining Rome's famous Appian Way, sometimes bore inscriptions in which slaves briefly expressed their feelings.

Aqueducts, like this one that crosses a major roadway leading into the Roman capital, were regularly maintained by gangs of slaves.

that the slaves in the state gang are paid for their work out of the state treasury, "an expense which is lightened by the receipt of rentals from water-rights." The slaves in the emperor's gang, on the other hand, are paid "from the emperor's privy purse [imperial finance office], from which are also drawn all expenses" for the upkeep of the aqueducts.[107]

Though the information Frontinus provides about the slaves in his charge is useful and important, it comes, as is so often the case, from the lofty vantage of a nobleman looking down on inferiors. It tells nothing about the slaves as human beings, how they felt about their jobs, their boss, their families, or life in general. For these insights, we must rely on the sparse contents of scattered surviving inscriptions. One, found on the tomb of one of the emperor's aqueduct workers, manages, despite its brevity, to deliver across the great gulf of time a message as meaningful now as it was then—heartfelt pride in work and family:

> To the spirits of the dead. Sabbio, slave of our Emperor, manager of the Claudian Aqueduct, made this for himself and for his wife Fabia Verecunda, with whom he lived faithfully for twenty-four years, and for his freedmen and freedwomen, and for their under-slaves [*vicarii*], and for all their descendants.[108]

CHAPTER 5

Striving for Acceptance: Manumission and the Contributions of Freedmen

One of the most important aspects of Roman slavery, from both social and economic standpoints, was manumission, the freeing of slaves. A slave granted liberty, or *libertas*, appropriately became known as a *libertus* (freedman) or *liberta* (freedwoman; in English, the term freedmen often denotes both men and women). These terms were used in reference to an ex-slave as an individual, while the terms *libertinus* and *libertina* described them as members of a social class. Thus, Tiro, Cicero's former slave, could be described either specifically as Cicero's illustrious *libertus*, or more generally as a Roman *libertinus*.

Freedmen had existed in Roman society since early republican times. But their numbers and social prominence were relatively insignificant until Roman masters began freeing some of the masses of slaves taken as war captives in the third and second centuries B.C. After that, *libertini* could be found in nearly every social and occupational niche, often taking jobs freeborn Romans did not want and routinely working alongside both slaves and the freeborn. In the late Republic, states Susan Treggiari, an authority on Roman freedmen, some *libertini* gained considerable influence thanks to "highly placed patrons or supporters, or wealth—or both." At the same time, she says,

humbler freedmen acquired a better position than before because of the new importance of trade and industry, in which they played a far more important role than did free-born Romans as subordinates and managers. . . . In this context, freedmen became commoner and more important to all classes of society, as artisans, as agents in business ventures, in private life, [and] in the civil service.[109]

As these conditions continued to prevail, manumission became an important means of upward social mobility for slaves; although only up to a point, for most freeborn Romans refused to accept ex-slaves as complete equals, no matter how talented, loyal, or honest they might be. Yet in spite of this barrier, freedmen strongly desired and consistently strove to be accepted in Roman society. And their talents, skills, and hard work contributed significantly to Rome's economic prosperity and cultural development. The profound and lasting effects of manumission on Roman society constitute perhaps the most positive feature of its slavery institution.

Various Modes of Manumission

Roman slaves achieved freedom in a number of ways. Many bought it using their *peculium*, and evidence suggests that some were so eager to increase their savings for this purpose that they periodically starved themselves so

This relief adorns the tomb of a well-to-do Roman and shows him flanked by two of his trusted freedmen.

that they could sell portions of their food rations for a profit. The price a slave had to pay for manumission no doubt varied widely. But it is likely that the master wanted back at least the amount he had originally paid for the slave. A master may also have demanded an added sum to help defray his costs of feeding and clothing the slave during the time he had owned him or her. Or the price of freedom might be met by other means than money, as in the case of some masters' manumitting female slaves who had produced a certain number of children (who were automatically the slaves of those masters). One such master was Columella, who wrote:

> To women . . . who are unusually prolific, and who ought to be rewarded for the bearing of a certain number of offspring, I have granted exemption from work and sometimes even freedom. . . . To a mother of three sons exemption from work was granted; to a mother of more her freedom as well.[110]

Another common way slaves gained their freedom was when kind masters granted it as a reward for years of loyalty and good service. Mutual affection and even genuine feelings of brotherly or fatherly love might also be involved, as in the case of Cicero and Tiro. Another of Cicero's letters expressing concern over his former slave's illness includes these words: "For myself, I long for your presence,

Another of the many later representations of Cicero, whose favorite freedman, Tiro, later wrote the great orator's biography.

but it is as one who loves you; love urges 'Let me see you in good health'; longing [urges] 'let it be with all speed.'"[111] Other masters manumitted slaves in open recognition of their obvious intellectual and literary talents, for at least a few Romans were genuinely ashamed to keep in servitude people culturally superior to themselves. Suetonius cites several examples, including that of Lucius Plotus, who

> is said to have been a slave and even to have served as a doorkeeper in chains . . . until he was set free because of his talent and interest in letters. . . . Then becoming a teacher of rhetoric [persuasive public speaking], he had [the illustrious military leader] Pompey the Great for a pupil, and wrote a history of [Pompey's] exploits. . . . He was the first of all freedmen to take up the writing of history, which up to that time had been confined to men of the highest position.[112]

Aulus Gellius mentions still another way that masters could transform their *servi* into *liberti*— by adopting them; although he cautions that social custom frowns on extending to such adoptees all of "the privileges of the freeborn."[113] Or a master might simply free a slave on a whim or for purely personal reasons. A parody of such manumission occurs in the *Satyricon* after a slave boy accidentally falls on Trimalchio, injuring his arm; Trimalchio frees the lad on the spot, "so that no one can say that so exalted a personage had been injured by a slave."[114]

Formal and Informal Ceremonies

Actually, Trimalchio would have needed to follow up with some sort of official ceremony, either formal or informal, to make the manu-

---

Manumission in the Master's Will

These manumission clauses are from the will (dated A.D. *191, quoted in Lewis and Reinhold's* Roman Civilization: Sourcebook II) *of a Roman naval veteran named Gaius Longinus Castor, a resident of Egypt.*

"I direct that my slave Marcella, over thirty years of age, and my slave Cleopatra, over thirty years of age, shall be freed, and that they shall each in equal portion be my heirs. . . . They shall enter upon the inheritance, each on her own portion, as soon as each thinks proper to attest that she is my heir, and it shall not be lawful to sell or mortgage it. But if the aforesaid Marcella suffers the lot of human kind [i.e., dies], then I wish her portion of the inheritance to go to [the slaves] Sarapio and Socrates and Longus. Similarly, in the case of Cleopatra, I wish her portion to go to Nilus. . . . My slave Sarapias, daughter of my freedwoman Cleopatra, shall be freed, and I give and bequeath to her five *arourae* [about 2½ acres] of grain land which I own in the vicinity of the village of Caranis . . . likewise one and one-quarter *arourae* of a ravine, likewise one-third portion of my house . . . likewise one-third portion of a palm grove which I own close to the canal called the Old Canal."

---

mission legal. The standard formal way was for the master and slave to stand before a public magistrate; the master held the slave's head and said words to the effect of "I desire this man (or woman) to be free," then removed his hands, symbolically "letting go" of his legal grasp over the slave; after which, the magistrate touched the slave with his rod (*vindicta*). The freedman then donned the *pilleus*, a felt cap symbolizing his freedom (ironically the same kind of cap placed on the heads of some slaves at slave auctions).

Perhaps more common were informal methods of manumission. For instance, a master could write a letter declaring his slave free. Or a master could announce a slave's emancipation in front of friends who acted as witnesses (called *inter amicos*, literally "among friends"). The following excerpt is from a surviving "deed," drawn up in A.D. 221 in Roman Egypt, to ensure the legality of an *inter amicos* manumission:

> Marcus Aurelius Ammonio, son of Lupercus . . . and Terheuta, of the ancient and illustrious [city of] Hermopolis Major, manumitted in the presence of friends his house-born female slave Helene, about thirty-four years old, and ordered her to be free, and received for her freedom from Aurelius Ales, son of Inarous, of the village of Tisichis . . . 550 *denarii*, which the said Ales . . . made a present of to the aforementioned freedwoman Helene. Done [agreed to] at Hermopolis Major . . . July 25 . . . year 4 of the Emperor Elagabalus [signatures of Ammonio and Ales are attached].[115]

Having shed their slave status, freedmen received new names from their former masters. The standard method was to assign the freedman the master's given name (*praenomen*), followed by the master's clan name (*nomen*), followed by the freedman's original slave name. Thus, once freed by Marcus Tullius Cicero, the slave Tiro became the freedman known as Marcus Tullius Tiro. In all formal documents, freedmen were also required to insert the letter *l.*, which stood for *libertus*, and it was customary to precede this with the genitive form of the master's *praenomen* to indicate who had freed him or her. Tiro's official written freedman name, therefore, was Marcus Tullius Marci libertus Tiro, customarily abbreviated as M. Tullius M. l. Tiro.[116] Freedmen's children born after their parents' liberation dropped the *l.*, since they were born free, and usually also dropped their parents' slave names to help conceal their servile heritage.

Manumission by Last Will and Testament

All of these forms of manumission occurred when the master was still living. On the other hand, a number of masters provided in their wills that when they died some or all of their slaves would become free, a process known as *manumissio testamento*. In a will dated to A.D. 142, for example, a soldier named Antonius Silvanus included this manumission clause:

> As for my slave Cronio, after my death, if he has performed all his duties properly and has turned over everything to my heir above-named or to my trustee, then I desire him to be free, and I desire the five-percent manumission tax to be paid for him out of my estate.[117]

The motives for choosing this method were sometimes selfish. By announcing beforehand his intentions, a master might hope to instill gratitude in his slaves, who would, presumably, then give him more faithful service in his remaining years. Petronius poked fun at this common ploy by having Trimalchio make a dramatic announcement at his banquet:

"To make a long story short, I'm freeing all of them [my slaves] in my will. To Philargyrus, I'm leaving a farm, and his bed-fellow, too. Carrio will get a tenement house. . . . I announce all this in public so that my household will love me [now] as well as they will when I'm dead." They all commenced to pay tribute to the generosity of their master, when he, putting aside his trifling, ordered a copy of his will brought in, which same he read aloud from beginning to end, to the groaning accompaniment of the whole household.[118]

Yet other masters chose *manumissio testamento* out of the heartfelt belief that it was the right and generous thing to do for slaves who had given them so many years of hard work and devoted service. This attitude is reflected in a letter in which Pliny the Younger addresses the problem of a recently deceased friend who had neglected to free her slave in her will:

To Statius Saninus: I understand from your letter that Sabina, in making us her heirs, left us no instructions that her slave

Self-Restraint Rather than Insults

Among the most famous excerpts from the letters of Pliny the Younger is this one, in which he discusses dining with his freedmen, suggesting that at least some upper-class Romans extended to ex-slaves the same respect and courtesy they themselves expected.

"It would take too long to go into the details . . . of how I happened to be dining with a man . . . whose elegant economy, as he called it, seemed to me a sort of stingy extravagance. The best dishes were set in front of himself and a select few, and cheap scraps of food before the rest of the company. . . . One lot was intended for himself and for us, another for his lesser friends (all his friends are graded), and the third for his and our freedmen. My neighbor at table noted this and asked me if I approved. I said I did not. 'So what do you do?' he asked. 'I serve the same to everyone, for when I invite guests it is for a meal, not to make class distinctions; I have brought them as equals to the same table, so I give them the same treatment in everything.' 'Even freedmen?' 'Of course, for then they are my fellow-diners, not freedmen.' 'That must cost you a lot.' 'On

Pliny the Younger, the government official and prodigious letter-writer, was an unusually enlightened slave owner.

the contrary.'. . . Believe me, if you restrain your greedy instincts it is no strain on your finances to share with several others the fare you have yourself. It is this greed which should be put down and 'reduced to the ranks' if you would cut down your expenses, and you can do this far better by self-restraint than by insults to others."

Modestus was to be given his freedom, but even so left him a legacy in the words, "To Modestus, whom I have ordered to be set free.". . . It seems to me obvious that it was a mistake on Sabina's part, and I think we ought to act as if she had set out in writing what she believed she had written. . . . Once understood, it should be legally binding on an honest heir, as honor puts us under an obligation as binding as necessity is for other people. Let us then allow Modestus to have his liberty and enjoy his legacy as if Sabina had taken every proper precaution. She did indeed do so by her wise choice of heirs.[119]

On another occasion, Pliny is "particularly pleased to hear that" his wife's grandfather "took the opportunity . . . to liberate a number of" his slaves in his will.[120] Pliny may have been more of a humanitarian than most Roman masters. However, his attitude about manumission was not uncommon. As the distinguished scholar A. M. Duff comments, Pliny "assumes that his correspondents are capable of appreciating his conduct [toward slaves] and that they follow the same rules in their own lives. Genuine charity, therefore, must have been a living force throughout the whole society with which he was intimate."[121]

Bound by Restrictions and Obligations

Whether a slave received freedom via the master's will or by some other method, he or she could look forward to some of the benefits enjoyed by freeborn Romans. The word "some" must be emphasized, for *libertini* faced certain restrictions that made them less free and of a distinctly lower status than the freeborn. First, a freedman was still bound to the former master under the rules of patronage, the social system in which a "client," or dependent person, owed loyalty and social respect (*obsequium*) to his or her "patron," or benefactor. "The figure of father and patron ought always to be respected and sacred in the eyes of a freedman or a son," states a jurist in Justinian's *Digest*. The same jurist adds that "a freedman who does not show due gratitude should not be allowed to get away with it." For the first such offense, a stiff warning is sufficient, but for a second or "if he has behaved insolently [toward] or abused" the patron and his family, "he should be punished, perhaps even with a period of exile."[122] Indeed, on occasion the state intervened to put a freedman in his place, redefining and upholding the obligations of *liberti* to patrons. According to Suetonius, the emperor Claudius enacted the rule that if a freedman "proved ungrateful to his former master and caused him annoyance, back he went into slavery."[123]

In addition to showing *obsequium*, a freedman also had the obligation of performing certain services, or *operae*, for his or her patron for a specified number of days each year. Usually, the freedman agreed to do so under oath immediately following the manumission ceremony. The *Digest* states: "He has an obligation to swear to provide work, gifts, or services; the work can be of any kind whatever, so long as it is imposed in an honorable, just, and legal way."[124] Thus, while custom obliged a former slave to perform duties for his or her patron, it also set limits on how much work the patron could demand; for instance, such work could not be so extensive as to prevent the freedman from earning a living. Scholar Peter Howell describes some typical services rendered to patrons by freedmen clients (as well as by freeborn clients):

Parted Only by Death

Often, the only way historians know about specific Roman freedmen and their lives is through funerary inscriptions, like this especially touching one found in the tomb of the Memmii in Rome (quoted in Wiedemann's Greek and Roman Slavery*).*

"In honor of Aulus Memmius Clarus: Dedicated by Aulus Memmius Urbanus to his fellow-freedmen and dearest companion. I cannot remember, my most respected fellow-freedmen, that there was ever any quarrel between you and me. By this epitaph, I invoke the gods of heaven and of the underworld as witnesses that we first met on the slave-dealer's platform, that we were granted our freedom together in the same household, and that nothing ever parted us from one another except the day of our death."

The patron could claim the client's support on those occasions when he felt his status required a numerous entourage—for instance in the law courts, at elections, at literary recitations, or even in his own dining room. By [the early Empire] a client seems to have been expected to call to greet his patron in the early morning, and accompany him on his social or business round, receiving at the end a small money "dole," or, if he was lucky, an invitation to dinner. . . . All this could, of course, be very tedious and time-consuming. The client . . . might have to walk long distances through crowded and muddy streets, up and down the hills of Rome, to reach his patron's house, and then most of the day might be wasted in trailing around from one boring occupation to another.[125]

Social and legal rules of patronage set certain other restrictions and penalties on freedmen. A freedman could not sue his former master, for example. In some cases the patron and/or patroness (and their immediate descendants) had a legal right to half of the estates of their *liberti*. Further, a freedman who attacked and injured a patron might be sentenced to work in the mines; and for committing adultery with the patron's wife, the sentence could be death.

Despite such drawbacks, the patron-client relationship benefited freedmen in various ways. A freedman could expect to receive not only periodic dinner invitations from a patron, but also legal protection or assistance; and neither the patron nor the freedman was required to give evidence against the other in court (except in treason cases). L. P. Wilkinson describes other benefits:

Often a freedman would go on living in the household of his patron, among people he knew and liked, perhaps in some responsible position such as butler or chef, secretary or tutor. Or the patron would set him up in business, perhaps on condition of sharing in the profits, or make him his political or business agent when he was abroad.[126]

Roman freedmen had to accept other social restrictions besides the patron-client relationship. They could not become senators; nor could they hold public office for the state or any town;[127] nor join the state priesthood (although they could be attendants to priests); nor serve as legionary soldiers or as Praetorian guards (the emperor's personal bodyguards). And typically, freedmen had to endure all manner of social inequities, such as sitting in lower seats and eating inferior food at upper-class dinner parties. These served as constant reminders of their servile origins.

Career Opportunities Open to Freedmen

The same sort of prejudice pertained to a freedman's choice of occupation, where "choice" did not have the same meaning as it did for freeborn persons. First, as Treggiari points out, in many cases a freedman's "choice must have been predetermined by his patron, either because he had been trained for some particular work, or because his patron in freeing him had some specific job in mind." [128] Also, as already seen, most freeborn Romans, particularly those with moderate or considerable means, viewed most kinds of menial, financial, and administrative jobs as degrading or unsuitable; so that these comprised the bulk of the positions open to slaves and freedmen.

The career avenues open to freedmen were therefore limited. And many must have found it difficult to refuse the offer of a comfortable position in the patron's household or business. A freedman who wanted to try going it alone might acquire a loan from the patron, set up a business, and then pay back the loan over time from the profits. Or, if the freedman's *peculium* was ample enough, he or she might be able to start a business without a loan. However, even these economically independent freedmen were still tied to their patrons, owing them *obsequii* and *operae*, and were no doubt grateful for any social, financial, or other favors their former masters might grant.

As to specific occupations, besides managers in the trades and industries and financial dealers, many *libertini* worked as scholars, teachers, scribes, and secretaries. Some, especially natives of Greece and Greek-speaking lands, had already been well educated before being enslaved through capture or sale. In many other cases, masters systematically educated *vernae* or other household slaves from childhood with the express idea of turning them into tutors, scholars, and secretaries. An outstanding example of a slave educated and then freed by a culture-conscious master was the renowned teacher Marcus Antonius Gnipho, whom Suetonius documents:

> It is said that he was a man of great talent, of unexampled powers of memory, and well-read not only in Latin but in Greek as well; that his disposition, too, was kindly and good-natured, and that he never made any stipulation about his fees, and therefore received the more from the generosity of his pupils. He first gave instruction in the house of the Deified Julius [Julius Caesar], when the latter was still a boy, and then in his own home. He taught rhetoric too, giving daily instruction in speaking. . . . They say also that distinguished men attended his school, including Cicero. [129]

Among many other such lettered freedmen were Parthenius, said to have taught the great Roman poet Virgil to read and write Greek, and Hyginus, whom Augustus placed in charge of the library on the Palatine Hill in Rome.

Freedmen were very common in other ocupations requiring substantial education, including doctor and architect. But many freedmen, and freedwomen too, worked alongside slaves and lower-class freeborn Romans in less prestigious professions. For instance, males were often laborers, as well as foremen, on construction sites; both males and females worked as entertainers, such as gladiators, actors, singers, dancers, and musicians; and probably a majority of prostitutes were freedwomen. In addition, freedwomen often performed as weavers, spinners, wool workers, and mill and bakery workers, although a few held more responsible or influential positions, such as landlady, moneylender, or shopkeeper.

Rising Influence

Public freedmen, especially in the civil services, were frequently the most visible and influential of their class. While they were excluded from holding public office, positions on the staffs of public officials were wide open to them. Once again, education was an important factor, for such jobs usually required reading, writing, and financial skills, as well as knowledge of Greek, all of which *libertini* possessed more often than humble freeborn Romans. Thus, it was not unusual for a freedman on an emperor's or governor's staff to wield considerably more influence and authority than most freeborn civil servants.

A number of such imperial freedmen became notorious, prompting A. M. Duff to remark that of all the nations in history, the Roman Empire "possesses the longest list of menials who rose to guide the destinies of state."[130] Among these were several who served the emperor Claudius. According to Tacitus, "Claudius now gave even ex-slaves, placed in

Many freedmen made their livings as entertainers, including musicians and puppeteers like those pictured here.

control of his personal estates, equal authority with himself and the law"; further, a freedman named Pallas became so influential at court that Claudius's successor, Nero, "deposed Pallas from the position from which, since his appointment by Claudius, he had virtually controlled the Empire."[131] Yet Nero himself depended a great deal on the shrewdness and negotiating skills of such highly placed freedmen. Faced with an overzealous governor and rebellious natives in Britain, Tacitus records, Nero sent the former imperial freedman Polyclitus

> to investigate the British situation. Nero was very hopeful that Polyclitus's influence would both reconcile the governor . . . and

pacify native rebelliousness. . . . Polyclitus . . . succeeded in intimidating even the Roman army. But the enemy laughed at him. For them . . . the power of ex-slaves was still unfamiliar. The British marveled that a general and an army that had completed such a mighty war should obey a slave.[132]

Many freeborn Romans deeply resented freedmen who managed to get rich and/or gain social and political influence. Tacitus, an upper-class gentleman, disdainfully suggested that such freedmen climbed the social ladder by taking advantage of the state's vulnerability in troubled times.[133] And Juvenal, of much humbler means, complained about "such

Claudius, the fourth Roman emperor, employed several freedmen who rose to positions of considerable power and influence in court circles.

In his Annals, *Tacitus tells the story of the failed conspiracy to assassinate the corrupt emperor Nero in A.D. 65, and how the freedwoman Epicharis, who was involved in the plot, courageously refused to reveal the names of her coconspirators.*

"Nero now remembered the information of Volusius Proculus [who had tipped him off about the plot] and consequent arrest of Epicharis. Thinking no female body could stand the pain, he ordered her to be tortured. But lashes did not weaken her denials, nor did branding—nor the fury of the torturers at being defied by a woman. So the first day's examination was frustrated. Next day her racked limbs could not support her, so she was taken for further torments in a chair. But on the way she tore off her breastband, fastened it in a noose to the chair's canopy, and placed her neck inside it. Then, straining with all her weight, she throttled the little life that was still in her. So, shielding in direst agony men unconnected with her and almost strangers, this former slavewoman set an example which particularly shone when free men, Roman knights and senators, were betraying, before anybody had laid a hand on them, their nearest and dearest."

men as Fortune, by way of a joke, will sometimes raise from the gutter and make Top People."[134] But while they might resent the occasional freedman who made good, most Romans recognized the fact that most freedmen were neither well-to-do nor influential and therefore posed no threat to the authority or dignity of the freeborn. The vast majority of *libertini* were poor, struggled along in unskilled or semiskilled jobs, and in death merged silently into Rome's masses of anonymous paupers' graves.

An Integral Role in Roman Life

Most Romans also recognized, if grudgingly, the abilities, talents, education, and other qualities of many thousands of ex-slaves of all walks of life. Such recognition can be seen in both individual slices of life and more general social realizations, ranging from the trust and friendship shared by Cicero and Tiro; to Pliny

A bust of Claudius's successor, the egotistical and brutal emperor Nero, whose misrule eventually prompted the Senate to brand him an enemy of the people.

the Younger's treatment of freedmen as equals at the dinner table;[135] to the readiness of generation after generation of Romans to entrust their children's welfare to freedmen tutors; to Tacitus's stirring description of a freedwoman whose courage and dignity surpassed that of men of his own class;[136] to the general realization, even by members of that privileged class, that freedmen and slaves often imparted much valuable knowledge and culture to their patrons and to society as a whole. These realities and countless thousands more like them made it clear that men and women who had once been slaves played an integral role in Roman life, and that Rome owed at least part of its success to their contributions.

Fear, Brutality, and Escape: The Darker Side of Roman Slavery

Much has been written, here and elsewhere, about slaves and masters getting along. Cited often is the kindness of owners like Pliny the Younger and the feelings of mutual respect and admiration between Cicero and Tiro. An important question is whether such cases constituted the rule or the exception in ancient Rome; and, unfortunately, the answer is not completely clear. Evidence suggests that humane treatment of slaves became increasingly common as the numbers of slaves and freedmen rose sharply in the late Republic. Clearly, though, not all masters were as thoughtful and lenient as Pliny, or as cultured and principled as Cicero; and rough and abusive treatment of slaves was not always confined to the mines and farm prisons. Abundant evidence shows that there was a darker, meaner, more sadistic side to Roman slavery. Perhaps inhumane, brutal masters were in the minority, but they nonetheless existed throughout Roman history. And that fact, coupled with the basic inequity and indignity of slavery as an institution, created an undercurrent of fear and tension that ran always just beneath the surface of slaves' everyday lives.

Yet the slaves were not the only ones who were afraid. The first-century A.D. playwright and philosopher Seneca recorded:

> On one occasion a proposal was made by the Senate to distinguish slaves from free men by their dress; it then became apparent how great would be the impending danger if our slaves began to count our [small] numbers [and their large ones].[137]

The rejection of this proposal was only one example of masters' fear of their slaves, which matched and sometimes exceeded slaves' fear of their masters. Other examples from the late Republic and early Empire include the extreme reluctance to allow slaves access to weapons and a ban on slaves' serving in the army, where they would receive both weapons and combat training.[138] Deep-rooted fear and hostility was also reflected in common adages, such as "You have as many enemies as you have slaves," and variations such as "A hundred slaves equals a hundred enemies." Even Pliny was not immune to this fear, as demonstrated in his reaction to hearing of a master murdered by slaves: "There you see the dangers, outrages, and insults to which we [the slave owners] are exposed. No master can feel safe because he is kind and considerate."[139] From a modern vantage, it might seem as though such worries and fears of Roman masters were largely groundless. After all, very few were murdered by their slaves; and at no time did violence by slaves, even in the large slave uprisings of late republican times, including that led by Spartacus, seriously threaten the Roman state or society as a whole. However, at the time these fears were both real and common.

A fanciful depiction of the slave leader Spartacus and some of his followers. His rebellion, the largest and most famous in Roman history, has been a frequent subject of modern literature, music, and films.

On a more positive note, some powerful Romans balanced worries for their own safety with genuine sympathy for abused slaves. And as a result, over time rulers enacted various laws aimed at safeguarding slaves from such abuse. Just how often these laws were invoked and how much they actually improved the quality of slaves' lives, however, is debatable.

Examples of Physical Abuse

One problem the framers of such laws faced was defining what constituted abuse of slaves and what should be accepted as "necessary" and "reasonable" discipline and punishment. Nearly all slaves suffered occasional punishment, even by the fairest and kindest masters. Besides assignment to extra work details, thrashings with rods or whips, and confinement to stocks, the most common penalty for minor offenses consisted of tying a slave's arms to a *furca*, a heavy forked log. Having to carry this burden around the house or street for hours or all day, the culprit, or *furcifer* (a term that came to mean "rascal"), suffered both physical discomfort and humiliation. As Varro and Columella attested, unruly farm slaves often spent time in the *ergastulum*. But particularly troublesome members of the *familia rustica* might be sentenced to days, weeks, or longer at the dreaded task of grinding in a flour mill. In *The Golden Ass*, Apuleius describes these poor wretches:

> Their entire bodies formed a pattern of livid bruises. Their backs, which bore the marks of the whip, were not so much covered as shaded by torn shirts of patchwork cloth. . . . They had . . . half-shaved heads, and chains round their ankles. Their faces were a ghastly yellow, and their eyes had contracted in the smoke-filled gloom of that steaming, dank atmosphere, making them half-blind. They resembled boxers who coat themselves with dust when they fight, for their bodies were a dirty white from the oven-baked flour.[140]

The plays of Plautus and Terence are filled with references to such punishments. In Terence's *Girl from Andros*, for example, a master warns his slave, "If I catch you up to any of your tricks today . . . I'll have you beaten senseless and sent to the mill."[141]

Yet the vast majority of Romans, no doubt including most slaves and freedmen, saw these kinds of punishment as routine and expected modes of discipline rather than as abuse or cruelty. It is somewhat unclear how they defined cruelty by a master; but apparently starving, crippling, permanently disfiguring, and/or inflicting pain for sport or sadistic pleasure rather than for discipline came under this heading.

Diodorus tells, for instance, of a wealthy couple, Damophilus and Megallis, who were notorious for their cruelty to their slaves: "Because of his . . . savage character, there wasn't a single day on which . . . Damophilus didn't torture some of his slaves without just cause. His wife took equal pleasure in these insolent punishments and treated her maids and those slaves who were under her jurisdiction with great brutality."[142] Eventually, Diodorus states, the slaves could bear no more and turned on their master and mistress, providing the initial spark for the first of the great slave uprisings.

Discipline and Brutality

The second-century A.D. Greek physician Galen, who attended members of many upper-class households, including those of some emperors, found nothing wrong with a master's administering "as many strokes of a rod or whip as they wished" to their slaves. But he was deeply disturbed by some of the more serious abuses he documented. "There are other people who don't just hit their slaves," he wrote,

> but kick them and gouge out their eyes and strike them with a pen if they happen to be holding one. I have seen someone strike his slave in the eye . . . with one of the reeds we use to write with. . . . The emperor Hadrian struck one of his attendants in the eye with a pen. When he realized that [the slave] had become blind in one eye as a result of this stroke, he . . . offered to let him ask for any gift to make up for what he had suffered. When the victim remained silent, Hadrian again asked him to make a request of whatever he wanted. [The slave] declined to accept anything else, but asked for his eye back—for what gift could provide compensation for the loss of an eye?[143]

The second-century A.D. *Greek physician Galen (pictured) documented a number of cases of masters abusing their slaves, including an incident involving the emperor Hadrian.*

The Pollio and Secundus Cases

Perhaps the two most infamous cases of arbitrary cruelty to slaves were those of Vedius Pollio and Pedanius Secundus. According to Dio Cassius, Pollio became "very well known for two reasons, his wealth and his cruelty, so that he has even found a place in history. . . . He kept in tanks giant eels which had been trained to devour men, and he was in the habit of throwing to them those of his slaves whom he wished to put to death."[144]

By contrast, the Secundus case demonstrated the cruelty of the system rather than that of a specific master. According to ancient tradition, if a slave murdered a master, all other slaves in the household must be executed. Roman jurists later explained the rationale this way: "No household could be safe if slaves were not forced by the threat of danger to their own lives to protect their masters against enemies both internal and external."[145] This penalty was seen as so harsh that by late republican times it was only very rarely invoked; however, the fact that it might be invoked at any time remained a potent threat hanging above the heads of all slaves.

One of those times came in A.D. 61 when Secundus, the wealthy and prestigious prefect of the capital city, was murdered by one of his four hundred slaves. According to Tacitus, after all of these *familia urbana* were condemned to die, "a crowd gathered, eager to save so many innocent lives, and rioting began." The Senate convened to debate the matter and the conservative aristocrat Cassius Longinus put into words the paranoid fear that so many Roman masters still harbored:

A man who has held the consulship has been deliberately murdered by a slave in his own home. None of his fellow-slaves prevented or betrayed the murderer. . . . Exempt them from the penalty if you like. But then, if the City Prefect was not important enough to be immune, who will be? Who will have enough slaves to protect him if Pedanius's four hundred were too few? Who can rely on his household's help if even fear for their own lives does not make them shield us? . . . The only way to keep down this scum is by intimidation. Innocent people will die, you say. Yes . . . [and yet] exemplary punishment always contains an element of injustice. But individual wrongs are outweighed by the advantage of the community.[146]

This view prevailed and the Senate upheld the death sentence. As the four hundred men, women, and children marched toward the crosses erected for their crucifixion, huge angry

"Sadism, Pure and Simple"

In this excerpt from his fourteenth satire (Peter Green's translation), Juvenal rails against the arbitrary abuses of a cruel slave master.

"Take Rutilus, now: does his conduct encourage a lenient temper? A sense of restraint when dealing with peccadilloes [trivial offenses]? Does he hold that slaves are fashioned, body and soul, from the same elements as their masters? Not on your life. What he teaches is sadism, pure and simple: there's nothing that pleases him more than a good old noisy flogging, no siren song to compare with the crack of the lash. To his quaking household he's a monster, a mythical ogre, never so happy as when the torturer's there on the job, and some poor wretch who's stolen a couple of towels is being branded with red-hot irons. What effect on the young must he have, with his yen for clanking chains, for dungeons, and seared flesh, and field-gang labor camps?"

crowds converged in hopes of protecting them; but the emperor Nero called out his troops, who surrounded the condemned, and the executioners proceeded to carry out their grim task.

The facts that the Senate engaged in a passionate debate, that the populace loudly protested, and that later Roman writers so often singled out the incident confirms that the Secundus case was extreme and unusual. That the case of Pollio and his man-eating eels was just as unusual is shown in Seneca's reaction: "Who did not hate Vedius Pollio even more than his own slaves did, because he would fatten his eels on human blood? . . . The monster! He deserved to die a thousand deaths!"[147] And as Seneca recorded, the emperor Augustus was equally disturbed, on one occasion severely rebuking Pollio for his cruelty and pardoning a slave the man had condemned to the eels.[148]

Escape and Recapture

Yet even if such abuses and atrocities were rare, they underscored the atmosphere of mutual fear and the very real threat of violence and death that pervaded the master-slave relationship. Indeed, that threat, combined with less drastic but still serious physical and psychological abuse, was enough to prompt many slaves to attempt escape. Actually, it was usually not very difficult for a slave to escape a master. As Keith Hopkins points out, unlike American black slaves, most Roman slaves "had no distinguishing marks. . . . Both as slaves and as freedmen they could merge with the rest of the population. In a society without photographs it was fairly easy for slaves to run away."[149]

Yet a runaway slave, or *fugitivus*, was usually just as easily caught. In a society in which nearly everyone accepted the inevitability of slavery, few people, not even most fellow slaves, were likely to aid a *fugitivus*, for he was seen as a thief who had stolen his master's property, namely himself. Masters often offered rewards for capturing and returning runaways. "A boy named Hermon has run away," begins a reward poster found in Roman Egypt. "[He is] about 15, wearing a cloak and a belt. Anyone who brings him back will receive . . . 3 talents; anyone who gives information that he is at a shrine . . . 2 talents. . . . Whoever wishes is to inform the governor's officials."[150] Some masters also hired special detectives who specialized in catching *fugitivi*.

Still another factor that made recapture likely was the common habit of branding and/or collaring slaves who ran away often. Usually, the offender had the letter *F*, for *fugitivus*, branded onto the forehead. The metal collars riveted around slaves' necks often bore inscriptions identifying the owner, as a surviving example states, "I have escaped; arrest me; take me back to my master Zoninus and you will be rewarded with a gold piece."[151] Over time, the purpose of such collars became so universally understood that many bore the abbreviation "T.M.Q.F.," which stood for *Tene me quia fugio*, or "Arrest me since I am a fugitive."[152]

The penalties for running away and also for helping a *fugitivus* could be harsh. The recaptured slave returned in shackles to the master, who at the very least had him severely whipped and/or chained for an indefinite period. If the offender did not already bear a brand mark or collar, he likely received one or both now; while a repeat offender might be sentenced to certain death in the arena or mines. As for those who aided runaways, the law was clear: "Anyone who has hidden a runaway slave is guilty of theft. . . . Any person whatsoever who apprehends a runaway slave has an obligation to produce him in public."[153]

Rebellion Useless

On rare occasions, runaways banded together and fought back, initiating a full-scale rebellion. The three major Roman insurrections occurred within a span of about seventy years, the first two in Sicily, from ca. 139 to 132 B.C. and from 104 to 100 B.C., and the third in Italy, from 73 to 71 B.C. Their nature and tragic outcomes help explain why Roman slaves did not instigate such rebellions more often.

In the first large slave war, after Damophilus' and Megallis's cruelty forced their slaves to turn on them, slaves from neighboring farms joined them. Under a leader named Eunus, they ransacked the countryside, over time swelling in number to about seventy thousand and taking control of most of Sicily. Eventually, the Roman Senate sent an army, which starved the rebels into submission. The second rebellion in Sicily was led by the slaves Salvius and Anthenion, who managed to defeat the first Roman forces sent against them and to reduce many Sicilian towns to the brink of starvation. But they were unable to stand up to an army of some seventeen thousand battle-hardened Roman troops under the consul Manius Aquilius, who crushed them and restored order.

The last and most famous of the large slave rebellions, that of Spartacus, began when a group of slaves at a gladiator school in Capua, about a hundred miles south of Rome, escaped and began terrorizing the surrounding countryside. According to Plutarch, the slaves

> had done nothing wrong, but, simply because of the cruelty of their owner, were kept in close confinement until the time came for them to engage in combat. Two hundred of them planned to escape, but their plan was betrayed and only seventy-eight . . . managed to act in time and get away, armed with choppers and spits which they seized from some cookhouse.

Spartacus freed many slaves in central Italy, built a formidable army from their ranks, and defeated several small Roman armies sent against him. But he was no fool. As Plutarch says, "He could not hope to prove superior to the whole power of Rome, and so he began to lead his army towards the Alps. His view was that they should cross the mountains and then disperse

A Man of Spirit, Strength, and Intelligence

Here, from his Life of Crassus (*in* Plutarch: Fall of the Roman Republic), *Plutarch tells how the last of the major slave rebellions began and offers some personal information about its famous leader.*

"The rising of the gladiators and their devastation of Italy, which is generally known as the war of Spartacus, began as follows. A man called Lentulus Batiatus had an establishment [training school] for gladiators at Capua. Most of them were Gauls and Thracians. They had done nothing wrong, but, simply because of the cruelty of their owner, were kept in close confinement until the time came for them to engage in combat. Two hundred of them planned to escape, but their plan was betrayed and only seventy-eight, who realized this, managed to act in time and get away, armed with choppers and spits which they seized from some cookhouse. On the road they came across some wagons which were carrying arms for gladiators to another city, and they took these arms for their own use. They then occupied a strong position and elected three leaders. The first of these was Spartacus. He was a Thracian from the nomadic tribes and not only had a great spirit and great physical strength, but was, much more than one would expect from his condition [i.e., slavery], most intelligent and cultured, being more like a Greek than a Thracian. They say that when he was first taken to Rome to be sold, a snake was seen coiled round his head while he was asleep and his wife . . . declared that this sign [omen] meant that he would have a great and terrible power which would end in misfortune. This woman shared his escape and was then living with him."

Spartacus meets his end at the hands of Roman troops. Spartacus was an inspiring leader and, according to the historian Plutarch, an intelligent and cultured individual.

towards their own homes, some to Thrace [in northern Greece] and some to Gaul."[154]

However, Spartacus's followers, having grown overconfident, refused to continue their northward march, preferring to continue ravaging central Italy. This proved their undoing. The government appointed the wealthy aristocrat Marcus Crassus to lead a large army against the rebellious slaves, and in 71 B.C. he caught up with them in the southern Italian region of Lucania. There, Spartacus and his followers staged a heroic last stand, but they ultimately went down to defeat. Spartacus and most of his followers died in the battle, and the six thousand surviving slaves were crucified along the road to Rome as a warning to others who might contemplate rebelling.

The lesson of these insurrections, in which a total of over a million slaves died, was clear to the slaves of succeeding generations. As Spartacus himself had realized, slave armies were not large, well trained, or well armed enough to stand up to the entire Roman military establishment, which was the most formidable in the world. They also lacked the organization and unity of all slaves, a factor essential to any hope of success, for none of these rebellions were class struggles

The survivors of Spartacus's slave army suffer crucifixion after the collapse of his rebellion. Thereafter, Roman history witnessed no more large-scale slave uprisings.

or attempts to free all slaves and abolish slavery. Most of Spartacus's followers, for example, at least at first, simply wanted to escape Italy and return to their homelands. And in the Sicilian uprisings, many slaves, especially *vernae*, refused to join the rebels and fought alongside their masters. The lesson for later Roman slaves, therefore, was that it was useless to rebel; and indeed, Spartacus's revolt was the last large slave uprising in Roman history.

"We Make Them Enemies"

Because slave runaways rarely succeeded and slave rebellions always failed, slaves had no viable way of avoiding the threat and reality of harsh treatment; and since they had no political voice whatsoever, they could not even attempt to reform the system. Luckily, the first two centuries A.D. witnessed the initiation of a number of reforms influenced by the slow but steady spread of more humanitarian views among the slave owners themselves. Pliny the Younger, of course, was an outstanding proponent of such views.

However, Seneca's advocacy of fair and humane treatment of slaves was perhaps the most expressive and enduring of the period. In his essay *On Anger*, he lectures that a free person reduced to slavery by capture deserves pity, not contempt.[155] He also calls upon masters to be less arrogant and to control their tempers:

> What right have I to [whip and chain] my slave for too loud a reply, too rebellious a look, a muttering of something that I do not quite hear? Who am I that it should be a crime to offend my ears? Many [great soldiers and rulers] have pardoned their enemies; shall I not pardon the lazy, the careless, and the babbler?[156]

Seneca, an adviser to the emperor Nero, was a humane, sensitive man who urged Roman slave masters to control their tempers.

Seneca is even more liberal and charitable in his epistle *On Master and Slave*:

> I am glad to learn . . . that you live on friendly terms with your slaves. This befits a sensible and well-educated man like yourself. "They are slaves," people declare. Nay, rather they are men. "Slaves!" No, comrades. "Slaves!" No, they are unpretentious friends. "Slaves!" No, they are our fellow-slaves, if one reflects that Fortune has equal rights over slaves and free men alike.

Fear, Brutality, and Escape: The Darker Side of Roman Slavery **79**

About the old adage that a master has as many enemies as he has slaves, Seneca maintains, "They are not enemies when we acquire them; we make them enemies," and then continues:

> Kindly remember that he whom you call your slave sprang from the same stock, is smiled upon by the same skies, and on equal terms with yourself breathes, lives, and dies. . . . This is the kernel of my advice: Treat your inferiors as you would be treated by your betters. . . . "He is a slave." His soul, however, may be that of a free man. "He is a slave." But shall that stand in his way? Show me a man who is not a slave; one is a slave to lust, another to greed, another to ambition, and all men are slaves to fear.[157]

One must be careful not to read too much into or overestimate the influence of Seneca's lofty pronouncements about the humanity of slaves. For one thing, he at no time advocated abolishing slavery, which he, like everyone else in his time, saw as natural and inevitable. He was merely arguing for better treatment. Nor is it likely that most slave owners were as liberal thinking as he, for after all, the senators who approved the pitiless execution of Secundus's four hundred slaves were Seneca's peers. Yet as Michael Grant points out, Seneca's writings at least "show that liberal views were in the air . . . for certainly, in [his] time, there was an increasing recognition of the *moral* personality of slaves."[158]

Laws Protecting Slaves

This recognition of slaves' humanity was reflected not only in the outrage of the crowds who protested the Secundus executions, but also in a series of laws passed in the early Em-

Antoninus's Decrees

This excerpt from Gaius's Institutes *(quoted in Lewis and Reinhold's* Roman Civilization: Sourcebook II*) summarizes some of the decrees of Antoninus Pius intended to protect slaves.*

"At the present time neither Roman citizens nor any other persons who are under the rule of the Roman people are permitted to treat their slaves with excessive and baseless cruelty. For, by enactment of the Emperor Antoninus, a man who kills his own slave without cause is ordered to be held just as liable as one who kills another's slave. And even excessive severity of masters is restrained by enactment of the same emperor. For, when consulted by certain governors of provinces about those slaves who seek asylum in temples of the gods or at statues of the emperors, he ordained that if the cruelty of the masters is found to be intolerable they are to be compelled to sell their slaves."

pire. Suetonius records a decree of the emperor Claudius in A.D. 47 that addressed the problem of masters abandoning their sick slaves:

> Finding that a number of sick or worn-out slaves had been marooned by their owners on the Island of Aesculapius in the Tiber [River], to avoid the trouble of giving them proper medical attention, Claudius freed them all and ruled that none who got well again should return to the control of his former owner; furthermore, that any owner who made away with [killed] a sick slave, rather than abandon him, should be charged with murder.[159]

Although Claudius emphasized that such murder charges applied only in cases of sick slaves, the idea of prosecuting a master for killing a slave under any circumstances was unprecedented and controversial.

Later emperors extended such protection to healthy slaves. First, Hadrian (reigned 117–138) forbade masters from killing their slaves, saying that such punishment could only be meted out by the courts. He stopped short of calling these masters murderers. However, his successor, Antoninus Pius (reigned 138–161), did so in a roundabout way; he said that "a man who kills his own slave without cause is ordered to be held just as liable as one who kills another's slave."[160]

Since the owner of a slave killed by another master had the choice of prosecuting the killer for murder, Antoninus's law allowed for the prosecution of a master who killed his own slave. Later, in the early fourth century, affected by the growing influence of Christian leaders, the emperor Constantine the Great was much more direct and specific, declaring that a master would be prosecuted for homicide if

he willingly kills [his slave] with a stroke of a cane or stone; inflicts a lethal wound by using something which is definitely a weapon; orders him to be hung from a noose; gives the shocking command that

The emperor Hadrian, one of the so-called "five good emperors" who ruled in the second century, initiated important legislation concerning slavery, including a law forbidding masters from killing their slaves.

he should be thrown down from a height; pours poison into him . . . or [kills him] by forcing [his] weakened limbs, running with blood and gore, to give up their life spirit as the result of torture—a form of brutality appropriate to savage barbarians.[161]

Other imperial decrees intended to protect slaves included one by Nero (under Seneca's urging) allowing slaves in Rome to appeal alleged mistreatment to the city prefect; a similar one by Antoninus Pius allowed slaves to appeal to local town judges, who could enforce their sale to kinder masters; one by Hadrian abolished private slave dungeons; another by Hadrian provided that when a slave killed a master, the only other household slaves subject to punishment should be those close enough to see or hear the crime; and one by Constantine forbade slave families breaking up during a sale.

These and other similar laws passed during the Empire were highly enlightened and progressive for their time, and indeed for any slave-owning society in history. However, the mere fact of their passage did not ensure systematic better treatment for all slaves. While the creation of such laws reflected the growth of humanitarian attitudes among Roman slave masters, it is questionable how many masters rigidly adhered to these rules; moreover, it is unlikely that more than a handful of those who broke them were actually prosecuted. As Hopkins suggests:

We should understand the laws as reflecting a desire of the ruling class to see that the worst excesses of masters were checked. . . . Ideals no doubt affected practice; but moral

Constantine the Great (pictured) forbade the branding of slaves on the face, having been convinced by his Christian advisers that doing so was an affront to God, who had supposedly fashioned human faces in his own image.

Saved from the Lash

In this brief episode from Petronius's Satyricon, *the story's heroes manage to save a slave from a serious flogging.*

"All of a sudden a slave, who had been stripped [in preparation for a beating], threw himself at our feet, and commenced begging us to save him from punishment, as it was no serious offense for which he was in jeopardy; the steward's clothing had been stolen from him in the baths, and the whole value could scarcely amount to ten *sestertii*. So we . . . intervened with the steward . . . begging him to remit the slave's punishment. Putting a haughty face on the matter, he said, 'It's not the loss I mind so much, as it is the carelessness of this worthless rascal. He lost my dinner clothes, given me on my birthday they were, by a certain client. . . . But what does it amount to? I make you a present of the scoundrel!' We felt deeply obligated . . . and the same slave for whom we had interceded rushed up to us as we entered the dining-room, and to our astonishment, kissed us . . . voicing his thanks for our kindness."

prescription is usually weak evidence of actual behavior. Evidence . . . suggests that laws and social values deprecating cruelty failed to prevent [all] excesses.[162]

Thus, while the philosophical views of men like Seneca and the imperial decrees of well-meaning rulers must have helped to improve the lives of slaves, fear and brutality remained realities of the slavery institution. History has shown time and again that corruption and abuse are bound to exist in any elite culture of slave owners. The only way the Romans could have completely eliminated these problems would have been to abolish slavery altogether. But this they never did.

The Decline of European Slavery

The massive and entrenched institution of slavery that had helped to support Roman civilization throughout much of Europe eventually died out. This did not occur through abolition, for despite some improvement in the treatment of slaves, thanks to changing attitudes and various imperial decrees, the Romans made no attempt to abolish slavery. Nor did slavery end through the replacement of slaves by free wage earners. Instead, a cheap labor force of serfs replaced the cheap labor force of slaves, a gradual process that continued well past the fall of the western Roman Empire in the late fifth century.

Mutual Obligations and the Status Quo

As to why the Romans never abolished slavery, nor for that matter even considered the idea, the simplest answer is that they saw no reason to do so. They did not view the idea of one person owning another as wrong, and their occasional intellectual debates about slavery centered mainly around the issues of cruelty, fair treatment, and social obligations. This is illustrated by the humanitarian attitudes voiced in the writings of Romans like Pliny the Younger and Seneca. They stressed the master's moral obligation to show restraint and moderation, and, conversely, the slave's obligation to show a fair and just master obedience; in short, they called for mutual understanding and duties within the framework of the status quo.

The situation was no different in the last two centuries of the Empire, when Christianity gained a guiding influence over Rome's government and society. As M. I. Finley points out, this period witnessed "not a trace of legislation designed to turn away from slavery, not even by gradual steps."[163] Keith Bradley adds:

> Clearly there was no Christian objection to owning slaves, whatever the teachings of the faith on spiritual equality. The Christian slaveowner was concerned to profit from the labor of his slave just like any other slaveowner, and he responded to what he perceived as criminal behavior in the slave in exactly the same way as his non-Christian counterpart.[164]

To rationalize their positions, Christian slave owners fell back on the letters of the early Christian leader Paul, who in writing about slaves emphasized the same themes as his contemporaries Pliny and Seneca. According to Paul, masters and slaves had mutual obligations on earth and would receive appropriate rewards or punishments later, in heaven:

> Slaves, obey in everything those who are your earthly masters . . . in singleness of heart, fearing the Lord. Whatever your task, work heartily, as serving the Lord and not men, knowing that from the Lord

you will receive the inheritance [of eternal life in heaven] as your reward. . . . Masters, treat your slaves justly and fairly, knowing that you also have a Master in heaven.[165]

Indeed, although Christian leaders consistently lobbied for humane treatment of slaves, they accepted slavery as a fact of life and their teachings may actually have strengthened, rather than discouraged, the institution. According to Professor Bradley:

> With the argument that obedience was to be given to them "as unto Christ," Christian slaveowners gave themselves a stronger grip on their slaves than they had ever had before. To pious slaves the teachings on obedience and submission automatically foreclosed all possibility of agitating for freedom . . . [or] of resisting servitude. Freedom of the spirit and hopes of eternal life, they were repeatedly told, were all that mattered. It was better to be the slave of an earthly master than to be the slave of sin. Slavery was the will of God.[166]

From Slaves to Serfs

Thus, despite the ascendancy of Christianity in late Roman times, when barbarian tribes overran the western Empire in the fifth and sixth centuries, the slavery institution was still in place in former Roman territories. Yet slavery was already on the decline, more from economic factors than from moral or philosophical ones. This was mostly the result of a rise in both the numbers and importance of *coloni*, poor tenant farmworkers, in the late Empire. The term *colonus* had originally meant simply a farmer or "rustic." Later, the word came to describe a tenant farmer working someone else's land, as in the case of a free *vilicus* managing an absentee landlord's estate. But by the last centuries of the Empire, *coloni* had became "tied" tenants, locked within an agricultural form of patronage (*patrocinium*). Professor Finley provides this definition: "In return for protection and a measure of relief, the peasant accepted the personal authority of a landlord (or landlord's agent) over himself and his holding, hence the loss of what remained of his independence."[167] Indeed, *coloni* became so dependent on and in debt to their landlords that they were routinely referred to as "slaves of the soil." Though not yet serfs in the medieval sense, since they had no obligation of military service, these poor tenant workers were, as Michael Grant says, "virtually serfs—not exactly slaves, but foreshadowing the serfdom of the Middle Ages."[168]

By Compulsion, Not Choice

Indebted tenant farmers were the key to the decline of European slavery; for their labor steadily replaced that of slaves, who became less and less necessary. The agricultural brand of *patrocinium* survived the fall of the western Empire and, in combination with other social and economic factors, slowly evolved into the medieval manorial system of lords and serfs. "The decline of slavery, in other words," Finley writes,

> was a reversal of the process by which slavery took hold. Once upon a time the employers of labor in these regions imported slaves to meet their requirements. Now their own lower classes were available, as they had not been before, by compulsion, not by choice, and so there

By the time the Frankish king Charlemagne was crowned, the European institution of slavery had largely died out.

was no need for a sustained effort to keep up the slave supply, nor to introduce wage-labor.[169]

And so, the dwindling numbers of slaves in the European kingdoms that grew on the Empire's wreckage slowly merged with and disappeared into the serf population; the process appears to have been more or less complete by the time the Frankish king Charlemagne was crowned Holy Roman Emperor in the year 800.

Ultimately, then, neither slave rebellions, nor class struggles, nor the moral arguments of philosophers, nor the triumph of Christianity, nor even the fall of Rome itself killed what had been the largest, most complex slavery institution in history. Instead, in the final analysis, Europe simply outgrew its need for slaves.

Notes

Introduction: The Nature of the Evidence

1. *Justinian Code*, 6.1.4.4, quoted in Alan Watson, *Roman Slave Law*. Baltimore: Johns Hopkins University Press, 1987, p. 131. The law codification ordered by the eastern emperor Justinian was completed between 528 and 534 and consists of three sections. The *Code* is a collection of former imperial statutes; the *Digest* is a collection of opinions and interpretations of these laws by eminent jurists; and the *Institutes* is a guide to the *Code* and *Digest* created for the use of law students. Relevant citations in these notes are marked accordingly.
2. Pausanias, *Guide to Greece*. 2 vols. Translated by Peter Levi. New York: Penguin, 1971, vol. 2, pp. 261–62.
3. Pliny the Elder, *Natural History*. 10 vols. Translated by H. Rackham. Cambridge, MA: Harvard University Press, 1967, 33.135.
4. Thomas Wiedemann, *Greek and Roman Slavery*. London: Croom Helm, 1981, p. 100.
5. Gaius, *Institutes*, quoted in Otto Kiefer, *Sexual Life in Ancient Rome*. New York: Dorset Press, 1993, p. 88.
6. Cicero, *De Officiis*. Translated by Walter Miller. Cambridge, MA: Harvard University Press, 1961, p. 191.
7. Keith Bradley, *Slavery and Society at Rome*. New York: Cambridge University Press, 1994, pp. 179–80.
8. Actually, Epictetus left no writings of his own. His ideas are preserved in the *Discourses* of his pupil, Arrian (the Greek historian who became famous for his *Anabasis*, a chronicle of the conquests of Alexander the Great).
9. A notable exception was the first-century B.C. freedman Publilius Syrus, who collected several common sayings, presumably coined by slaves and freedmen, among them: "It is beautiful to die instead of being degraded as a slave," and "If you don't like being a slave, you will be miserable; but you won't stop being a slave." (See Wiedemann, *Greek and Roman Slavery*, pp. 76–77, 111.)
10. Bradley, *Slavery and Society at Rome*, p. 180.

Chapter 1: The Brutal Reality of Supply and Demand: Becoming a Roman Slave

11. *Justinian Digest*, 1.5, quoted in Wiedemann, *Greek and Roman Slavery*, p. 15.
12. Gaius, *Institutes*, 1.9–11, quoted in Wiedemann, *Greek and Roman Slavery*, p. 24.
13. Aulus Gellius, *Attic Nights*. 3 vols. Translated by John C. Rolfe. Cambridge, MA: Harvard University Press, 1961, vol. 3, pp. 423–25.
14. The increasing importance of militarism in Roman life was the key factor. Most soldiers at this time were peasant farmers, the most likely candidates for debt-bondage. Since Rome needed all the soldiers it could get to facilitate its conquests, it was in the state's best interest to eliminate such servitude. The increase in captives and booty taken in these wars more than made up for the loss of cheap labor created by

the ban. See the comments of the first-century B.C. historian Livy in sections 6.27 and 8.28 of his famous history of Rome. (A noted translation of the complete work is that by Frank G. Moore. Cambridge, MA: Harvard University Press, 1966.)

15. Michael Grant, *A Social History of Greece and Rome*. New York: Charles Scribner's Sons, 1992, p. 101.

16. *Justinian Digest*, 1.5, quoted in Wiedemann, *Greek and Roman Slavery*, pp. 15, 23.

17. Modern historians estimate a similar ratio in the capital city of Rome: about 300,000 slaves out of a total population of approximately 1 million.

18. Pausanias, *Guide to Greece*, vol. 2, p. 189.

19. Suetonius, *Augustus*, in *The Twelve Caesars*. Translated by Robert Graves. New York: Penguin, 1989, p. 72.

20. Caesar promised the pirates that once they freed him he would punish them. They did not take this threat seriously, which proved a fatal mistake, for after his family paid the ransom of fifty talents (perhaps $300,000 or more in today's money), he returned with a company of troops, captured the surprised brigands, and eventually crucified them.

21. Though there were no large wars of aggression and only a few minor civil discords, occasional small-scale conflicts, such as putting down rebellions, occurred, periodically providing fresh supplies of war captives. In the Jewish War (A.D. 66–70), for instance, the Romans captured and enslaved over one hundred thousand people.

22. Harold Johnston, *The Private Life of the Romans*. New York: Cooper Square Publishers, 1973, p. 103.

23. Bradley, *Slavery and Society at Rome*, p. 43.

24. This should not be seen as a reliable method of ascertaining slave nationalities. A slave recently born into the household or imported from a western province, for instance Gaul, might be called Pharnaces, perhaps because he was replacing the original slave of that name, who had died, or simply because the master liked the name.

25. Juvenal, *Satires*. Translated by Peter Green. New York: Penguin, 1974, pp. 92–93.

26. Horace, *Satires, Epistles, Ars Poetica*. Translated by H. Rushton Fairclough. Cambridge, MA: Harvard University Press, 1966, p. 33.

27. Petronius, *Satyricon*. Translated by W. C. Firebaugh. New York: Horace Liveright, 1927, p. 105.

28. Johnston, *The Private Life of the Romans*, p. 104.

29. Some prices quoted in ancient sources are given in *denarii*, while many others are in *sestertii*. Four *sestertii* equaled one *denarius*, and for the sake of clarity all of the figures quoted in this volume have been converted to *denarii*.

30. Petronius, *Satyricon*, p. 132. The reference to circumcision informs us that the slave was Jewish, since at the time the Jews were the only inhabitants of the Roman realm who systematically circumcised their male children.

31. F. R. Cowell, *Life in Ancient Rome*. New York: G. P. Putnam's Sons, 1961, p. 97.

Chapter 2: "Sir, I Do My Best": The Privileges and Perils of Household Slaves

32. M. I. Finley, *The Ancient Economy*. Berkeley and Los Angeles: University of California Press, 1985, pp. 18–19.

33. L. P. Wilkinson, *The Roman Experience*. Lanham, MD: University Press of America, 1974, p. 128.

34. Kenneth Hughes, *Slavery*. London: George Allen and Unwin, 1977, pp. 41–42.

35. For more extensive lists and discussions of such specialized servants, see Bradley, *Slavery and Society at Rome*, pp. 57–65; also see Susan Treggiari, "Domestic Staff at Rome During the Julio-Claudian Period," *Social History* 6 (1973): pp. 241–55, and "Jobs in the Household of Livia," *Papers of the British School of Rome* 45 (1975): pp. 48–77.

36. Johnston, *The Private Life of the Romans*, p. 113.

37. Juvenal, *Satires*, p. 167.

38. Horace, *Satires, Epistles, Ars Poetica*, p. 291.

39. See Cicero, *Letters to Atticus*. 3 vols. Translated by E. O. Winstedt. Cambridge, MA: Harvard University Press, 1961, 12.18.3, 12.21.4, 13.2.1, 13.12.4, 13.30.2, 13.50.5, 15.15.1.

40. Cicero to Tiro, November 7, 50 B.C., in Cicero, *Letters to His Friends*. 3 vols. Translated by W. Glynn Williams. Cambridge, MA: Harvard University Press, 1965, vol. 3, p. 325.

41. Pliny the Younger, *Letters*. Translated by Betty Radice. New York: Penguin, 1969, p. 152.

42. Apuleius, *The Golden Ass*. Translated by P. G. Walsh. Oxford: Oxford University Press, 1994, p. 34.

43. Statius, *Silvae*, in *Works*. 2 vols. Translated by J. H. Mozley. Cambridge, MA: Harvard University Press, 1961, pp. 335–37.

44. Plutarch, *Life of Pompey*, in Rex Warner, trans., *Plutarch: Fall of the Roman Republic*. New York: Penguin, 1972, p. 241.

45. Appian, *Civil Wars*, 4.43, in *Roman History*. 4 vols. Translated by Horace White. Cambridge, MA: Harvard University Press, 1964, vol. 4, pp. 213–15. (The *Civil Wars* constitutes a portion of Appian's larger history of Rome.)

46. There was even a Roman cult that worshiped the *Manes serviles*, or spirits of slaves' deceased ancestors.

47. In one of his satires (1.8.8), Horace describes slaves being buried in mass paupers' graves; however, this seems to be a reference to a very old and outdated custom. By his day, household slaves received decent burials and, quite often, inscribed memorials.

48. For a detailed discussion of the participation of slaves in such clubs, see W. W. Buckland, *The Roman Law of Slavery: The Condition of the Slave in Private Law from Augustus to Justinian*. New York: AMS Press, 1969, pp. 74–75.

49. Horace, *Satires, Epistles, Ars Poetica*, p. 229. Although the master in this piece is named Horace, he is not supposed to be the author himself. It must be kept in mind that this is a work of fiction and humor; the name of the slave, Davus, was a common one for slave characters in the late Greek and early Roman comic plays; and the various morsels of wisdom spouted by this Davus probably correspond more to the beliefs of the author, the real Horace, than to those of any particular slave. Nevertheless, the role reversal and Davus's forwardness are characteristic of Roman Saturnalia festivities.

50. Sarah B. Pomeroy, *Goddesses, Whores, Wives, and Slaves: Women in Classical Antiquity*. New York: Schocken Books, 1995, p. 193.

51. Tacitus, *Annals*. Translated by Michael Grant. New York: Penguin, 1989, p. 276.

52. A notable exception was the case of "fiscal" slaves, or those owned by the emperor (called fiscal because the ones who were paid received their money from the public treasury). These imperial slaves *were* allowed to marry free women. Their children acquired "Latin" citizenship, which was less prestigious than full Roman citizenship; however, there was ample room for upward mobility, as it was not difficult for Latins to become full citizens if they were so inclined. An excellent informative discussion of Roman and Latin citizenship appears in John Crook, *Law and Life of Rome*. Ithaca, NY: Cornell University Press, 1967, pp. 36–47.

53. R. H. Barrow, *Slavery in the Roman Empire*. New York: Barnes and Noble, 1996, pp. 101–102.

54. Terence, *Phormio*, in *Works*, published as *The Comedies*. Translated by Betty Radice. New York: Penguin, 1976, p. 229.

55. For Juvenal's description of a slave who "can afford to squander a senior officer's income on classy prostitutes," see *Satires*, p. 91 (3.131–34).

56. Petronius, *Satyricon*, p. 142.

57. See Ammianus Marcellinus, *History*, published as *The Later Roman Empire*, A.D. *354–378*. Translated and edited by Walter Hamilton. New York: Penguin Books, 1986, 22.4.9–10.

58. Petronius, *Satyricon*, p. 143.

59. For instance, Plutarch, *Life of Cato*, 24, in Ian Scott-Kilvert, trans., *Plutarch: Makers of Rome*. New York: Penguin, 1965, pp. 146–47.

60. Salvian, *On the Governance of God*, quoted in Wiedemann, *Greek and Roman Slavery*, p. 179.

61. Apuleius, *The Golden Ass*, pp. 147–48; also see Suetonius, *Nero*, 11, in *The Twelve Caesars*, pp. 218–19, an example of an emperor frivolously giving slaves away to his guests at a celebration.

62. See Jane F. Gardner, *Women in Roman Law and Society*. Indianapolis: Indiana University Press, 1986, pp. 139–141.

63. Terence, *The Girl from Andros*, in *The Comedies*, p. 71.

Chapter 3: A Tool Endowed with Speech: Slavery on a Roman Farm

64. Garry Wills, ed., *Roman Culture: Weapons and the Man*. New York: George Braziller, 1966, p. 24.

65. These were the major products of Italian farms during the heyday of Roman slavery (ca. 200 B.C.–A.D. 200). By this era, the growing of wheat and other grains had ceased to be profitable in Italy; most were imported from fertile grain-producing regions in the provinces of Africa, Egypt, and Gaul.

66. A. H. M. Jones, "Slavery in the Ancient World," in M. I. Finley, ed., *Slavery in Classical Antiquity*. New York: Barnes and Noble, 1968, p. 8.

67. Pliny the Younger, *Letters*, pp. 105–106.

68. Columella, *On Agriculture*. 3 vols. Translated by H. B. Ash et al. Cambridge, MA: Harvard University Press, 1960, vol. 1, pp. 81–83.

69. Columella, *On Agriculture*, vol. 1, p. 83.

70. Evidently very few *vilici* were freedmen, although it appears that some freedmen worked their former masters' lands as tenants or visited the estates periodically in various capacities at the bequests of these masters. For opinions and discussion, see A. M. Duff, *Freedmen in the Early Roman Empire*. Oxford: Clarendon Press, 1928, p. 93; and Susan Treggiari, *Roman Freedmen During the Late Re-*

public. New York: Oxford University Press, 1969, pp. 106–10.

71. Cato, *On Agriculture*, quoted in Wiedemann, *Greek and Roman Slavery*, p. 149.
72. Columella, *On Agriculture*, vol. 1, p. 85.
73. Quoted in Wiedemann, *Greek and Roman Slavery*, p. 150.
74. Quoted in Wiedemann, *Greek and Roman Slavery*, p. 150.
75. See Cicero, *Against Verres*, published as *Verrine Orations*. 2 vols. Translated by L. H. G. Greenwood. Cambridge, MA: Harvard University Press, 1966, vol. 2, 3.50.19. In prosecuting Verres, a provincial governor, for corruption, Cicero compared him to a dishonest *vilicus*; though this description of a farm manager cheating his master was stated in the hypothetical sense, the implication was that such incidents were well known.
76. Columella, *On Agriculture*, vol. 3, pp. 191–93.
77. Columella, *On Agriculture*, vol. 1, p. 97.
78. Columella, *On Agriculture*, vol. 1, pp. 97–99.
79. Varro, *On Landed Estates*, quoted in Wiedemann, *Greek and Roman Slavery*, pp. 146–47.
80. Columella, *On Agriculture*, vol. 1, pp. 99–101.
81. Varro, *On Landed Estates*, quoted in Wiedemann, *Greek and Roman Slavery*, p. 139.
82. Cato, *On Agriculture*, quoted in Wiedemann, *Greek and Roman Slavery*, p. 184.
83. Plutarch, *Life of Cato*, in *Plutarch: Makers of Rome*, p. 143.
84. Plutarch, *Life of Cato*, in *Plutarch: Makers of Rome*, p. 125.
85. See Pliny the Younger, *Letters*, p. 106.
86. Particularly unruly city slaves were sometimes punished by temporary confinement in the master's farm dungeon.
87. Columella, *On Agriculture*, vol. 1, pp. 94–95.
88. Columella, *On Agriculture*, vol. 1, p. 95.
89. Quoted in Wiedemann, *Greek and Roman Slavery*, p. 76.

Chapter 4: "Vulgar" but Indispensable: Slaves in Business and Public Service

90. Cicero, *De Officiis*, p. 153.
91. Grant, *A Social History of Greece and Rome*, p. 100.
92. Keith Hopkins, *Conquerors and Slaves: Sociological Studies in Roman History. Vol. 1.* New York: Cambridge University Press, 1978, p. 124.
93. Barbers (*tonsores*) also occupied permanent positions on the household staffs of many wealthy Romans; and there were also itinerant, or traveling, barbers, who were almost always slaves. While men patronized barbershops, women had their hair done at home, usually by slaves.
94. Juvenal, *Satires*, p. 69. The phrases "four hundred thousand" and "qualify for the gentry" refer to property qualifications of the upper classes. Admission to the gentry, or Equestrian Order (also Knights), made up of well-to-do businessmen, required a minimum net worth of 400,000 *sestertii* (100,000 *denarii*).
95. Quoted in Barrow, *Slavery in the Roman Empire*, p. 116.
96. Quoted in Barrow, *Slavery in the Roman Empire*, p. 106.
97. Bradley, *Slavery and Society at Rome*, p. 76.
98. Quoted in Barrow, *Slavery in the Roman Empire*, p. 107.

99. See Mima Maxey, *Occupations of the Lower Classes in Roman Society*. Chicago: University of Chicago Press, 1938, pp. 89–90.

100. Diodorus Siculus, *Library of History*, vol. 3. Translated by C. H. Oldfather. Cambridge, MA: Harvard University Press, 1961, pp. 195–97, 199–201. Diodorus here specifically refers to privately owned silver mines in Iberia (Roman Spain).

101. Michael Grant, *Gladiators*. New York: Barnes and Noble, 1995, p. 31.

102. See J. P. V. D. Balsdon, *Life and Leisure in Ancient Rome*. New York: McGraw-Hill, 1969, p. 302, for conjecture about gladiators receiving freedom on retirement.

103. Hopkins, *Conquerors and Slaves*, pp. 123–24.

104. Pliny the Elder, *Natural History*, 29.8.19, quoted in Wiedemann, *Greek and Roman Slavery*, p. 73.

105. Most of the information we have about them comes from inscriptions on tombs and monuments and from references in legal documents, particularly those commissioned by Justinian.

106. Frontinus, *The Aqueducts of Rome*. Translated by Charles E. Bennett. Cambridge, MA: Harvard University Press, 1961, pp. 427–29, 447–49.

107. Frontinus, *The Aqueducts of Rome*, pp. 449–51.

108. Quoted in Wiedemann, *Greek and Roman Slavery*, p. 165. Sabbio shared the tomb with Sporus, another slave-manager of the Claudian Aqueduct.

Chapter 5: Striving for Acceptance: Manumission and the Contributions of Freedmen

109. Treggiari, *Roman Freedmen During the Late Republic*, p. 244.

110. Columella, *On Agriculture*, vol. 1, p. 95.

111. Cicero to Tiro, November 3, 50 B.C., in Cicero, *Letters to His Friends*, vol. 3, p. 319.

112. Suetonius, *On Rhetoricians*. Translated by J. C. Rolfe, in *Works*. 2 vols. Cambridge, MA: Harvard University Press, 1965, vol. 2, p. 443.

113. Aulus Gellius, *Attic Nights*, vol. 1, p. 439.

114. Petronius, *Satyricon*, p. 113.

115. Quoted in Naphtali Lewis and Meyer Reinhold, eds., *Roman Civilization: Sourcebook II: The Empire*. New York: Harper and Row, 1966, p. 262.

116. To this general rule there were a number of exceptions and variations. See Duff, *Freedmen in the Early Roman Empire*, pp. 52–58, and Treggiari, *Roman Freedmen During the Late Republic*, pp. 250–51.

117. Quoted in Lewis and Reinhold, *Roman Civilization: Sourcebook II*, p. 280.

118. Petronius, *Satyricon*, p. 136.

119. Pliny the Younger, *Letters*, p. 117.

120. Pliny the Younger, *Letters*, p. 207.

121. Duff, *Freedmen in the Early Roman Empire*, p. 100.

122. Quoted in Wiedemann, *Greek and Roman Slavery*, p. 53.

123. Suetonius, *Claudius*, in *The Twelve Caesars*, p. 201.

124. Quoted in Wiedemann, *Greek and Roman Slavery*, p. 55.

125. Peter Howell, Introduction, to Martial, *Epigrams*. Translated by James Michie. New York: Penguin, 1978, pp. 12–13.

126. Wilkinson, *The Roman Experience*, p. 132.

127. The exception was in the colonies established in Greece, Spain, and elsewhere by Julius Caesar during his dictatorship in the 40s B.C.; evidently Caesar was more approving of and generous in treating freedmen; they became so numerous and important in these colonies that they

were allowed to continue serving as local magistrates there after his death.

128. Treggiari, *Roman Freedmen During the Late Republic*, p. 87.
129. Suetonius, *Grammarians*, in Rolfe, trans., *Works*, vol. 2, p. 407.
130. Duff, *Freedmen in the Early Roman Empire*, p. 174.
131. Tacitus, *Annals*, pp. 279, 289.
132. Tacitus, *Annals*, pp. 331–32.
133. See Tacitus, *Histories*. Translated by Kenneth Wellesley. New York: Penguin, 1993, p. 64.
134. Juvenal, *Satires*, p. 88.
135. See Pliny the Younger, *Letters*, pp. 63–64.
136. See Tacitus, *Annals*, p. 373.

Chapter 6: Fear, Brutality, and Escape: The Darker Side of Roman Slavery

137. Seneca, *On Mercy,* in *Moral Essays*. 3 vols. Translated by John W. Basore. Cambridge, MA: Harvard University Press, 1963, vol. 1, p. 421.
138. The exception, of course, was gladiators, many of whom were slaves; however, gladiators were strictly supervised, they mostly trained with wooden weapons, and they had to surrender their real weapons immediately after fighting in the arena.
139. Pliny, *Letters*, p. 101; this remark directly contradicts one he makes earlier in the same letter, when he admits that the murdered man, Larcius Macedo, "was a cruel and overbearing master," suggesting that Pliny is here reacting emotionally to a fear pervasive among his peers.
140. Apuleius, *The Golden Ass*, pp. 168–69.
141. Terence, *The Girl from Andros*, in *The Comedies*, p. 47.
142. Diodorus, *Library of History*, quoted in Wiedemann, *Greek and Roman Slavery*, p. 203.
143. Galen, *The Discourses of the Mind*, quoted in Wiedemann, *Greek and Roman Slavery*, pp. 180–81.
144. Dio Cassius, *Roman History*. Translated by Ian Scott-Kilvert. New York: Penguin, 1987, p. 175.
145. *Justinian Digest*, 29.5.1, quoted in Wiedemann, *Greek and Roman Slavery*, p. 169.
146. Quoted in Tacitus, *Annals*, pp. 333–34.
147. Seneca, *On Mercy*, in *Moral Essays*, vol. 1, p. 409.
148. See Seneca, *On Anger*, in *Moral Essays*, vol. 1, p. 349; and see also Dio Cassius, *Roman History*, pp. 175–76.
149. Hopkins, *Conquerors and Slaves*, p. 121.
150. Quoted in Wiedemann, *Greek and Roman Slavery*, p. 192.
151. Quoted in Hopkins, *Conquerors and Slaves*, p. 121.
152. Quoted in Wiedemann, *Greek and Roman Slavery*, p. 194.
153. *Justinian Digest*, 11.4.1, 3, quoted in Wiedemann, *Greek and Roman Slavery*, p. 190.
154. Plutarch, *Life of Crassus*, in *Plutarch: Fall of the Roman Republic*, p. 122, 123–24.
155. See Seneca, *On Anger*, in *Moral Essays*, vol. 1, pp. 327–29.
156. Seneca, *On Anger*, in *Moral Essays*, vol. 1, pp. 315–17.
157. Seneca, Epistle 47, *On Master and Slave*, in *Moral Epistles*. 3 vols. Translated by Richard M. Gummere. Cambridge, MA: Harvard University Press, 1961, vol. 1, pp. 301–303, 307, 311.
158. Grant, *A Social History of Greece and Rome*, p. 106.
159. Suetonius, *Claudius*, in *The Twelve Caesars*, p. 201.

160. Gaius, *Institutes*, quoted in Lewis and Reinhold, *Roman Civilization: Sourcebook II*, p. 269.

161. *Theodosian Code*, 9.12.1, quoted in Wiedemann, *Greek and Roman Slavery*, p. 174.

162. Hopkins, *Conquerors and Slaves*, pp. 122–23.

Epilogue: The Decline of European Slavery

163. Finley, *The Ancient Economy*, p. 88.

164. Bradley, *Slavery and Society at Rome*, p. 147.

165. Colossians 3:22–25, 4:1, in Bible, Revised Standard Version.

166. Bradley, *Slavery and Society at Rome*, p. 151.

167. M. I. Finley, *Ancient Slavery and Modern Ideology*. New York: Penguin, 1980, p. 146.

168. Grant, *A Social History of Greece and Rome,* pp. 90–91; helping to confirm this scenario is the fact that, by the fifth and sixth centuries, the word *servus*, which had originally meant a slave, had come to mean a serf, too.

169. Finley, *The Ancient Economy*, p. 93.

Glossary

a cyatho: A cupbearer.

a lagona: A flagon or pitcher holder.

a purpuris: A servant in charge of purple garments.

a vesta privata: An emperor's servant in charge of palace garments; **a vesta forensi**, city clothes; **a vesta castrensi**, informal military uniforms; **a vesta triumphali**, full-dress parade uniforms; **a vesta gladiatoria**, theater clothes.

aediles: Roman officials who oversaw slave auctions, maintained roads, and organized public games.

analectae: Busboys (or girls) who cleaned up after a banquet.

anteambulones: In a retinue (a group of slaves accompanying a master and/or mistress when outside the house), slaves who cleared the way.

arator: A plowman.

architectus: An architect.

argentarius: A silversmith.

aroura (pl. arourae): A land measure used in Roman Egypt, equal to just over half an acre.

atriensis: In early Roman times a household's head slave; later, a butler.

aurifex: A goldsmith.

balneatores: Bathhouse attendants.

capsarius: A clothes folder.

client: In the Roman patronage system, a dependent person who owed loyalty and services to a benefactor (patron), who provided legal and other protection in return.

coci: Cooks.

collegia funeraticia: Burial clubs that paid the funeral expenses of members.

colonus (pl. coloni): A free tenant farmer; in later Roman times, such tenants became serfs known as "slaves of the soil."

contubernium (pl. contubernia): "Cohabitation"; a slave marriage, not recognized as legal by Roman law.

decuriae: Divisions of ten household slaves each.

denarius (pl. denarii, Eng. slang "dinars"): A common unit of Roman money.

dispensator: A head accountant or financial manager.

dominica potestas: The legal power of a master over his slaves.

dominium: The power of a *paterfamilias* over his possessions (including slaves).

dominus: Lord.

domus: A town or city house.

dulciarii: Sweetmeat preparers.

ergastulum: A farm prison.

familia: The Roman household or family.

familia rustica: Farm slaves.

familia urbana: Household slaves.

fornacarii (or fornacatores): Furnace operators.

fosseres: Farmworkers who specialized in digging furrows and ditches.

freedman (or freedwoman): A freed slave.

fugitivus (pl. fugitivi): A runaway slave.

furca: "Fork"; a heavy forked log to which a person's arms were tied; Roman slaves commonly carried the *furca* as a punishment.

furcifer: One who carried a *furca*; a rascal or troublemaker.

institor (pl. institores): A person, slave or free, appointed by a business-owner to manage that business.

inter amicos: "Among friends"; a mode of manumission in which a master freed a slave in the presence of friends, who acted as witnesses.

lanipendus: A wool weigher.

lares: Household spirits thought to keep the home safe.

latifundium (**pl.** *latifundia*): A large country ranch or landed estate worked mainly by slaves.

lectica: A litter, usually carried by slaves.

libarii: Pastry cooks.

libertas: Freedom.

libertinus (**f.** *libertina*, **pl.** *libertini*): A freedman, used when describing him as a member of a social class.

libertus (**f.** *liberta*, **pl.** *liberti*): A freedman, used when describing him as an individual or in relation to his former master.

magister: Master.

mancipia: Property consisting of slaves.

manu capiantur: Force of arms, as in war.

manumissio testamento: A mode of manumission in which a master freed a slave through a clause in his will.

manumission: The process of freeing a slave.

manus: The power of a *paterfamilias* over his wife and sons' wives.

Matronalia: A Roman holiday, celebrated on March 1, in which a household's mistress switched places with her slave attendants.

ministratores: Waiters.

nomen: A Roman's clan name.

nomenclator: A slave who reminded a master of people's names.

obsequium (**pl.** *obsequii*): An obligation of loyalty and respect owed by a freedman to his or her former master (now patron).

obstetrix: A midwife.

operae: Work, services, or duties owed by a freedman to his or her former master (now patron).

opiliones: Sheepherders.

ornator (**f.** *ornatrix*): A personal dresser.

ostiarius: A doorkeeper.

paedagogus: A slave who accompanied the master's son to school and supervised his behavior there.

pastores: Animal herders.

paterfamilias: The head of a Roman household.

patrocinium: "Protection" or "patronage"; in one context of the late Roman Empire, an agricultural relationship in which a free tenant submitted himself and his plot of land to the authority of a landlord, who in return provided legal and other kinds of protection.

patron: In the Roman patronage system, a free person, often well-to-do, who acted as benefactor and protector of a number of dependents (clients), who owed him loyalty and services in return.

peculium (**pl.** *peculia*): A slave's personal savings, consisting of money or property given to him or her by the master or earned outside the house by the slave.

pilleus (**or** *pilleum*): A cap placed on a slave's head during an auction, signifying that the seller offered no warranty on the slave; also, a felt cap worn by freedmen to symbolize their liberty.

pistor (**pl.** *pistores*): A combination of miller and baker.

pistrinum: A shop that sold bread.

potestas: The power of a *paterfamilias* over his children, grandchildren, and slaves.

praegustator: A food taster.

praenomen: A Roman's given or personal name.

procurator: An agent authorized by a master to transact business.

puer: Boy, often corrupted as "por" and used in the naming of slaves in early Roman times; for instance, the slave Marcipor was "Marcus's boy."

putatores: Farmworkers who specialized in pruning and trimming.

ratiocinator: An accountant.

rudiarius: A retired gladiator.

saltuarii: "Boundary keepers"; farmworkers who specialized in maintaining and guarding an estate's borders.

Saturnalia: A Roman holiday, celebrated in December, one of the customs of which was for a master and his slaves to switch places.

servus (pl. servi): A slave; *servi privati* were private slaves and *servi publici* were public slaves.

structores: Butlers who ordered an emperor's meals.

tector: A plasterer.

Tene me quia fugio: "Arrest me since I am a fugitive," the phrase often abbreviated as T.M.Q.F. on Roman slave collars.

titulus: A placard listing a slave's qualifications and serving as a warranty, hung around the slave's neck during an auction.

tonsor (pl. tonsores): A barber.

tonstrina: A barber shop.

triclinarii: Dining-room attendants.

verna (pl. vernae): A slave born and raised in the household.

vicarius (f. vicaria, pl. vicarii): The slave of a slave.

vilicus (f. vilica, pl. vilici): A farm manager, usually a slave.

vindicta: A rod, often a public magistrate's symbol of authority, with which the magistrate touched and thereby freed a slave during a formal manumission ceremony; also used to describe that particular mode of manumission.

vinitores: Vine dressers.

For Further Reading

Isaac Asimov, *The Roman Empire*. Boston: Houghton Mifflin, 1967. An excellent, easy-to-read, although brief and general, overview of all aspects of imperial Roman history, providing a good background for studies of everyday Roman life.

Lionel Casson, *Daily Life in Ancient Rome*. New York: American Heritage, 1975. A fascinating presentation of how the Romans lived: their homes, streets, entertainments, eating habits, and marriage customs, with numerous references to slaves and freedmen.

Charles Freeman, *The World of the Romans*. New York: Oxford University Press, 1993. This handsomely mounted volume, loaded with colorful photos and drawings, provides an excellent introduction to most of the important aspects of everyday Roman life and culture in both the Republic and Empire, including slavery. The text is nonscholarly and accessible to junior high and high school, as well as adult, readers.

Kenneth Hughes, *Slavery*. London: George Allen and Unwin, 1977. An accurate, informative, and very well-written brief introduction to both Greek and Roman slavery, explaining how people became slaves, their social status, the jobs they performed, their treatments, punishments, and so on.

Anthony Marks and Graham Tingay, *The Romans*. London: Usborne, 1990. Aimed at basic readers, this is a very accurate and entertaining summary of Roman history and life, with hundreds of fine color illustrations.

Don Nardo, *The Roman Republic* and *The Roman Empire*. San Diego: Lucent Books, 1994; *The Age of Augustus*, *The Punic Wars*, and *The Importance of Julius Caesar*. San Diego: Lucent Books, 1996; *The Collapse of the Roman Republic* and *The Roman Colosseum*. San Diego: Lucent Books, 1997; and *The Decline and Fall of Rome*. San Diego: Lucent Books, 1998. These comprehensive but easy-to-read volumes comprise a general overview of the important events and major political and military figures of Roman history, providing a useful background for the information in this volume about Roman slavery.

Works Consulted

Major Ancient Sources Consulted:

Author's Note: The best available general compilation of ancient documents about Roman slavery is Thomas Wiedemann, *Greek and Roman Slavery*. London: Croom Helm, 1981, from which I have quoted extensively. Included are excerpts from works by Appian, Gaius, Suetonius, Tacitus, Petronius, Pliny the Elder, Varro, and other classical writers, and also from inscriptions and the two great Roman law compilations, the Theodosian and Justinian Codes. Other ancient Roman laws and documents pertaining to slavery and related topics (as well as different translations of some of those quoted by Wiedemann) are found in Harries and Wood, *The Theodosian Code*; Buckland, *The Roman Law of Slavery*; Crook, *Law and Life of Rome*; Watson, *Roman Slave Law*; Barrow, *Slavery in the Roman Empire*; and Garnsey, *Social Status and Legal Privilege in the Roman Empire* (all six see below).

Of the key ancient works on Roman slavery, the more complete translations consulted and quoted include:

Columella, *On Agriculture*. 3 vols. Translated by H. B. Ash et al. Cambridge, MA: Harvard University Press, 1960. A native of Roman Spain, Columella was a first-century A.D. retired army officer and practical farmer. Luckily for posterity, his *On Agriculture*, a lengthy treatise on Roman agricultural techniques and the management of large estates, has survived and constitutes our most comprehensive source of information not only on these topics, but on the lives of Roman farm slaves as well.

Dio Cassius, *Roman History*. Translated by Ian Scott-Kilvert. New York: Penguin, 1987. A historian of the late second and early third centuries A.D., Dio wrote a history of Rome from its founding to the year 229. Of the original eighty volumes, about a third survive whole or in part, while some other sections were summarized by later ancient writers. Dio discusses Augustus's and Hadrian's regulations about manumission; the attitudes of the emperors Tiberius, Claudius, and Nero toward slaves; as well as slaves used in fire brigades and as rowers, marriage between slaves and free people, and more.

Petronius, *Satyricon*. Translated by W. C. Firebaugh. New York: Horace Liveright, 1927. Petronius was a first-century A.D. administrator, poet, and influential courtier to the corrupt emperor Nero. After becoming a suspect in one of the plots against the emperor, Petronius was ordered to commit suicide and spent his last hours compiling a list of Nero's most despicable acts. The *Satyricon* (or "Book of Satyr-like Adventures"), among the earliest versions of the western European novel, concerns the sexual misadventures of three young men—Encolpios, Ascyltos, and Giton. Literary scholar Charles Whibley writes of them: "They knew neither finery nor self-respect. . . . Home was as strange to them as a change of linen; they journeyed from inn to inn; and they were lucky if, after an evening's debauch, they found their resting-place, or escaped a brawl and a beating." Petronius's original work must have been very long, for the surviving fragments, apparently from volumes 14 to 16, are many thousands of words in length. Of main interest is the fascinating and often hilarious episode subtitled "Trimalchio's Feast," in which the main characters attend a sumptuous, overly gaudy banquet given by the rich but vulgar freedman Trimalchio. Although the plot is fiction and the situations often exaggerated or satiric, the institutions, customs, and character types described, a great many of them involving slaves and freedmen, are generally true to life. In his introduction to this edition, Firebaugh writes, "Nineteen centuries have gone their way since this novel was written, but if we look about us . . . we will find here, in a little corner of the Roman world, all humanity was held in miniature. Petronius must be credited with the great merit of having introduced realism into the novel."

Pliny the Younger, *Letters*. Translated by Betty Radice. New York: Penguin, 1969. A distinguished first-century A.D. senator, administrator, and letter writer, Pliny was the nephew and adopted son of the famous encyclopedist Pliny the Elder, as well as the trusted confidant of the emperor Trajan and friend of the noted writers Tacitus, Suetonius, and Martial. Pliny's letters reveal his attitudes about slavery, and also those of other well-to-do Romans, as well as valuable information about public slaves, slaves in the army, slaves used as dowry, the emperor's freedmen, exposure, manumission, and more.

Seneca, *Moral Epistles*. 3 vols. Translated by Richard M. Gummere. Cambridge, MA: Harvard University Press, 1961; and *Moral Essays*. 3 vols. Translated by John W. Basore. Cambridge, MA: Harvard University Press, 1963. Seneca (ca. 4 B.C.–A.D. 65) was a talented, urbane, and brilliant Stoic philosopher and playwright who served as tutor and court adviser to the notorious emperor Nero. Although Seneca is famous for urging humane treatment for slaves and preaching that slaves and free men were equal in the sight of the gods, he, like other ancient Stoics and Christians, stopped short of calling for the abolition of slavery. Whatever his personal opinion about slavery, Seneca's works, especially his epistles, are very valuable sources of information about ancient slavery.

Suetonius, *The Twelve Caesars*. Translated by Robert Graves. New York: Penguin, 1989. Suetonius, who lived from about A.D. 69 to 140, was a personal secretary of the emperor Hadrian as well as a noted biographer and historian. Though many of Suetonius's works are lost, his *Lives of the Twelve Caesars*, covering the rulers from Julius Caesar through Domitian, survives complete and is a valuable source of information about Rome in the late Republic and early Empire. Suetonius discusses Augustus's slavery laws, the attitudes of various emperors about slaves, the nationalities of slaves, the number of slaves in Rome, slaves used as farm laborers, and other aspects of the lives of slaves and freedmen.

Tacitus, *Annals*. Translated by Michael Grant. New York: Penguin, 1989; and *Histories*. Translated by Kenneth Wellesley. New York: Penguin, 1993. The works of Cornelius Tacitus (ca. A.D. 55–120), one of the greatest of all ancient historians, are particularly rich in references to and anecdotes about slaves and freedmen. He discusses their roles in the household of the emperor Tiberius, slavery laws passed by the emperor Claudius, the murder of Pedanius Secundus by a slave and subsequent execution of the other slaves in Secundus's household, private slaves used for public work, and a great deal more.

Other Translations of Ancient Works Consulted or Quoted:

Ammianus Marcellinus, *History*, published as *The Later Roman Empire, A.D. 354–378*. Translated and edited by Walter Hamilton. New York: Penguin Books, 1986.

Appian, *Roman History*. 4 vols. Translated by Horace White. Cambridge, MA: Harvard University Press, 1964.

Apuleius, *The Golden Ass*. Translated by P. G. Walsh. Oxford: Oxford University Press, 1994.

Cicero, *De Officiis*. Translated by Walter Miller. Cambridge, MA: Harvard University Press, 1961; *Letters to Atticus*. 3 vols. Translated by E. O. Winstedt. Cambridge, MA: Harvard University Press, 1961; *Letters to His Friends*. 3 vols. Translated by W. Glynn Williams. Cambridge, MA: Harvard University Press, 1965; and *Verrine Orations*. 2 vols. Translated by L. H. G. Greenwood. Cambridge, MA: Harvard University Press, 1966.

Diodorus Siculus, *Library of History*. Vol. 3. Translated by C. H. Oldfather. Cambridge, MA: Harvard University Press, 1961.

Frontinus, *The Aqueducts of Rome*. Translated by Charles E. Bennett. Cambridge, MA: Harvard University Press, 1961.

Aulus Gellius, *Attic Nights*. 3 vols. Translated by John C. Rolfe. Cambridge, MA: Harvard University Press, 1961.

Horace, *Satires, Epistles, Ars Poetica*. Translated by H. Rushton Fairclough. Cambridge, MA: Harvard University Press, 1966.

Juvenal, *Satires*. Translated by Peter Green. New York: Penguin, 1974.

Naphtali Lewis and Meyer Reinhold, eds., *Roman Civilization: Sourcebook I: The Republic* ; and *Roman Civilization: Sourcebook II: The Empire*. New York: Harper and Row, 1966.

Martial, *Epigrams*. Translated by James Michie. New York: Penguin, 1978.

Pausanias, *Guide to Greece*. 2 vols. Translated by Peter Levi. New York: Penguin, 1971.

Pliny the Elder, *Natural History*. 10 vols. Translated by H. Rackham. Cambridge, MA: Harvard University Press, 1967.

Plutarch, *Lives*. Excerpted in Rex Warner, trans., *Plutarch: Fall of the Roman Republic*. New York: Penguin, 1972; and Ian Scott-Kilvert, trans., *Plutarch: Makers of Rome*. New York: Penguin, 1965.

Polybius, *The Histories*. Translated by W. R. Paton. Cambridge, MA: Harvard University Press, 1966.

Statius, *Works*. 2 vols. Translated by J. H. Mozley. Cambridge, MA: Harvard University Press, 1961.

Suetonius, In *Works*. 2 vols. Translated by J. C. Rolfe. Cambridge, MA: Harvard University Press, 1965.

Terence, *Works*, published as *The Comedies*. Translated by Betty Radice. New York: Penguin, 1976.

Major Modern Sources Consulted:

R. H. Barrow, *Slavery in the Roman Empire*. New York: Barnes and Noble, 1996. In one of the better scholarly overviews of the subject, Barrow quotes extensively from Tacitus, Pliny the Younger, Petronius, Seneca, and other ancient writers who discussed slavery, and also provides a handy reference list of their pertinent works.

Keith Bradley, *Slaves and Masters in the Roman Empire: A Study in Social Control*. New York: Oxford University Press, 1987. A fine scholarly examination of the conditions under which slaves lived in the Empire, including slave families, manumission, and the occurrence and severity of abuse by masters.

————, *Slavery and Society at Rome*. New York: Cambridge University Press, 1994. Another excellent study by Bradley, this one focusing on what he calls the "central period" of Roman history, namely 200 B.C. to A.D. 200, thus encompassing the late Republic and early Empire; topics covered include the slave supply, types of slave labor, and how slavery affected the progress (or lack thereof) of Roman society.

W. W. Buckland, *The Roman Law of Slavery: The Condition of the Slave in Private Law from Augustus to Justinian*. New York: AMS Press, 1969. This is the most detailed and authoritative source for Roman slave law, but its extremely scholarly and dense text will be useful only to other scholars and/or advanced, serious students of Roman civilization.

F. R. Cowell, *Life in Ancient Rome*. New York: G. P. Putnam's Sons, 1961. This readable synopsis of Roman life contains an informative chapter on slavery, covering roughly the same ground as Kenneth Hughes's *Slavery* (see For Further Reading).

A. M. Duff, *Freedmen in the Early Roman Empire*. Oxford: Clarendon Press, 1928. An excellent scholarly examination of the lives, jobs, and social and legal status of Roman freedmen. Although a few more recent works serve to update and supplement this one, it remains the definitive general source on Roman freedmen.

M. I. Finley, ed., *Slavery in Classical Antiquity*. New York: Barnes and Noble, 1968. This thoughtful collection of articles and essays about ancient slavery by various widely respected scholars includes an especially good one by A. H. M. Jones, one of the twentieth century's greatest Roman historians.

M. I. Finley, *Ancient Slavery and Modern Ideology*. New York: Penguin, 1980. Finley, a fine scholar, pulls no punches in this discussion and critique of various modern interpretations of the evidence about ancient slavery. He shows, for instance, the weakness of the old argument that Christianity was a strong force working for the abolition of slavery in late classical times. Of interest mainly to scholars.

Michael Grant, *A Social History of Greece and Rome*. New York: Charles Scribner's Sons, 1992. One of the most prolific and popular of modern classical historians, Grant here provides a useful general overview of social relations in the ancient Mediterranean world, including chapters on serfs, slaves, and freedmen, as well as on the status of foreigners and the contrasting lives of the rich and poor.

Keith Hopkins, *Conquerors and Slaves: Sociological Studies in Roman History. Vol. 1.* New York: Cambridge University Press, 1978. A useful study of the impact of Rome's extensive military conquests on its political, social, and economic structure, with an emphasis on the many captives brought back as slaves.

Sarah B. Pomeroy, *Goddesses, Whores, Wives, and Slaves: Women in Classical Antiquity*. New York: Schocken Books, 1995. Pomeroy, a professor of classics at Hunter College, delivers a highly informative sketch of the roles of women in the Greek and Roman world. As the title suggests, various aspects of slavery are discussed, especially as the institution affected women.

Susan Treggiari, *Roman Freedmen During the Late Republic*. New York: Oxford University Press, 1969. This scholarly study of Roman freedmen concentrates on late republican times and can be used by serious Roman students as a supplement to Duff's authoritative volume (see above). Treggiari offers much useful data on the careers of freedmen (trade, industry, agriculture, arts, medicine, the theater, and so on) and also chapters on the religion and family life of freedmen. The quotations in this work are mainly in Latin and Greek, making it accessible primarily to scholars.

Alan Watson, *Roman Slave Law*. Baltimore: Johns Hopkins University Press, 1987. This volume was ably summarized in its review by the distinguished Stanford University scholar Susan Treggiari: "A succinct account of all facets of the Roman law of slavery, intended for ancient historians interested in Roman slavery, law, or society, as well as for scholars working in other disciplines and for students. Watson is one of the few authorities on Roman law writing in English, and this is one of the few books on Roman law accessible to the nonspecialist reader."

Additional Modern Sources Consulted:

J. P. V. D. Balsdon, *Life and Leisure in Ancient Rome*. New York: McGraw-Hill, 1969.

Arthur E. R. Boak, *A History of Rome to 565 A.D.* New York: Macmillan, 1943.

Keith Bradley, *Discovering the Roman Family: Studies in Roman Social History*. New York: Oxford University Press, 1991.

P. A. Brunt, *Italian Manpower, 225 B.C.–A.D. 14*. London: Cambridge University Press, 1971.

Averil Cameron, *The Later Roman Empire*. Cambridge, MA: Harvard University Press, 1993.

Jerome Carcopino, *Daily Life in Ancient Rome: The People and the City at the Height of the Empire*. New Haven, CT: Yale University Press, 1940.

Lionel Casson, *Daily Life in Ancient Rome*. New York: American Heritage, 1975.

John Crook, *Law and Life of Rome*. Ithaca, NY: Cornell University Press, 1967.

Jean-Michel David, *The Roman Conquest of Italy*. Translated by Antonia Nevill. London: Blackwell, 1996.

Donald R. Dudley, *The Romans: 850 B.C.– A.D. 337*. New York: Knopf, 1970.

M. I. Finley, *The Ancient Economy*. Berkeley and Los Angeles: University of California Press, 1985.

Charles Freeman, *Egypt, Greece and Rome: Civilizations of the Ancient Mediterranean*. Oxford: Oxford University Press, 1996.

Jane F. Gardner, *Women in Roman Law and Society*. Indianapolis: Indiana University Press, 1986.

Peter Garnsey, *Social Status and Legal Privilege in the Roman Empire*. Oxford: Clarendon Press, 1970.

Michael Grant, *The World of Rome*. New York: Penguin, 1960.

——, *History of Rome*. New York: Scribner's, 1978.

——, *Gladiators*. New York: Barnes and Noble, 1995.

Jill Harries and Ian Wood, eds., *The Theodosian Code*. Ithaca, NY: Cornell University Press, 1993.

Harold Johnston, *The Private Life of the Romans*. New York: Cooper Square Publishers, 1973.

A. H. M. Jones, *Decline of the Ancient World*. New York: Longman, 1966.

Otto Kiefer, *Sexual Life in Ancient Rome*. New York: Dorset Press, 1993.

Aaron Kirschenbaum, *Sons, Slaves, and Freedmen in Roman Commerce*. Washington, DC: Catholic University of America Press, 1987.

Mima Maxey, *Occupations of the Lower Classes in Roman Society*. Chicago: University of Chicago Press, 1938.

Chester G. Starr, *Civilization and the Caesars*. New York: W. W. Norton, 1965.

Paul Veyne, ed., *From Pagan Rome to Byzantium*. Vol. 1 of Philippe Ariès and Georges Duby, eds., *A History of Private Life*. Cambridge, MA: Harvard University Press, 1987.

P. R. C. Weaver, *Familia Caesaris: A Social Study of the Empire's Freedmen and Slaves*. London: Cambridge University Press, 1972.

William Westermann, *The Slave Systems of Greek and Roman Antiquity*. Philadelphia: American Philosophical Society, 1964. Note: Although this volume contains much valuable information, some of Westermann's conclusions have been challenged by other historians. For scholarly critiques, see P. A. Brunt, *Journal of Roman Studies* 48 (1958): 164–70; and G. E. M. de Ste. Croix, *Classical Review* 7 (1957): 54–59.

L. P. Wilkinson, *The Roman Experience*. Lanham, MD: University Press of America, 1974.

Garry Wills, ed., *Roman Culture: Weapons and the Man*. New York: George Braziller, 1966.

Index

Picture Credits

Cover photo: AKG, London

Archibald Cary Coolidge Fund, Courtesy, Museum of Fine Arts, Boston, 60 (top)

Archive Photos, 35, 57, 60 (bottom), 67, 69

Corbis, 81

Corbis-Bettmann, 10, 15, 29, 31, 41, 55, 58, 63, 72, 78

Courtesy, Museum of Fine Arts, Boston, 32

Library of Congress, 86

North Wind Picture Archives, 9, 13, 14, 16, 18, 23, 28, 30, 37, 51, 74, 82

Stock Montage, Inc., 19, 21, 26, 43, 48, 49, 52, 68, 77

Tony Stone Images, 39, 79

About the Author

Classical historian and award-winning writer Don Nardo has published more than twenty books about the ancient Greek and Roman world. These include general histories, such as *The Roman Empire, The Persian Empire,* and *Philip and Alexander: The Unification of Greece*; war chronicles, such as *The Punic Wars* and *The Battle of Marathon*; cultural studies, such as *Life in Ancient Greece, Greek and Roman Theater, The Age of Augustus,* and *The Trial of Socrates*; and literary companions to the works of Homer and Sophocles. Mr. Nardo also writes screenplays and teleplays and composes music. He lives with his lovely wife, Christine, and dog Bud on Cape Cod, Massachusetts.